Church and Worship in Fifth-Century Rome:

The Letter of Innocent 1 to Decentius of Gubbio

Text with Introduction, Translation and Notes

by

Martin F Connell

GROVE BOOKS LIMITED

RIDLEY HALL RD CAMBRIDGE CB3 9HU

Contents

THE EDITOR

Martin Connell is a Professor of Liturgics at St. John's University,
Collegeville, Minnesota, USA

THE COVER PICTURE

shows Innocent 1, a picture reproduced from Joseph S Brusher,
Popes through the Ages (Van Nostrand, Toronto, 1959) p 81

First Impression June 2002
ISSN 0951-2667
ISBN 1 85174 502 5

Historical Context

Though Rome was a long way from the eastern Mediterranean land where Jesus lived and where Christian communities were first founded, the New Testament bears witness that a community of the new faith existed in the city at least by the time the apostle Paul wrote his letter to the Romans about a quarter-century after the death of Jesus; he visited there a few years later.[1] The extant letter reveals how quickly the new faith spread to the western Mediterranean basin, but after Paul's letter further testimony about liturgical offices, ministries, or rites comes over a century later in the Apostolic Tradition of Hippolytus, whose Roman provenance is itself under investigation.[2]

In his letter to the Church at Rome, Paul mentioned church orders and roles, such as that of the 'deacon' Phoebe (16.1), of his 'co-workers' (16.3, 9, 12), some of whom were 'prominent among the apostles' (16.7), others designated as 'chosen' (16.13), 'brothers,' 'sisters,' 'family,' and 'saints.' He made no mention of 'bishops' or 'presbyters'—*episcopoi* or *presbyteroi*—in the relatively long missive to that community of believers so far from Palestine.

Though tradition has passed down, at least from the sixth-century *Liber pontificalis*, an episcopal lineage of Roman bishops, or 'overseers,' from the apostle Peter to the then current Bishop of Rome—therewith starting the construction of an 'unbroken' concatenation of leaders of the Roman Church—there is in reality not much historically reliable evidence for leaders of the Church of Rome in the second half of the first or first half of the second centuries. For many of the names on such lists, the only extant piece is a name.

Subsequent persecutions in the early centuries, from what is known of them from testimonies and excavations, had the Christians of Rome more occupied with survival than with accurate chronologies of their leaders for the memory of ecclesial generations in the Eucharistic prayers of ages to come. The early churches of the New Testament were ever vigilant for the advents of either aggressive civil authorities or their irenic risen Lord at his second coming (e.g., Romans 1.7b; 1 Thessalonians 4.13-17). But they did not share, for later Christian centuries, the confidence about the omnipresence of the faith and its hegemony in many Western cultures, conditions that would perhaps have secured the episcopal lineage more reliably.

Late evidence about the Church of Rome becomes more plentiful and

---

1   Hans Dieter Betz, 'Paul' in *Anchor Bible Dictionary*, volume 5 (Doubleday, New York, 1992) pp 186-201; Charles D. Myers, Jr., 'Romans, Epistle to' in *Anchor Bible Dictionary*, volume 5 (Doubleday, New York, 1992) pp 816-830.
2   See the commentary on *Apostolic Tradition* 21: 22 in P. Bradshaw, M. Johnson, and L.E. Phillips, *The Apostolic Tradition ascribed to Hippolytus*, Hermenia Commentary Series (Fortress Press, Minneapolis, 2002). For an accessible translation of this ancient church order of the early third century, see *Hippolytus: A Text for Students*, intro., trans., commentary, notes Geoffrey J. Cuming (Grove Books, Bramcote, 1976).

historically dependable with its rising prominence after the reign of the emperor Constantine, under whose rule the Church was granted freedom to exist and, eventually, thrive. On his own acceptance of the Christian faith near the end of his life (+337), Constantine built three basilicas in or near the city of Rome.

The Church in Rome today has had such vast and deep religious and liturgical, political and cultural influences on all seven continents that it is nearly impossible to imagine when the influence of the Roman Church was not so apparent and perhaps not so stable. But it was so for the first few centuries of the faith.

The episcopal letter of this investigation, translation, and commentary gives witness to a time when the Roman Church was on its way from being merely one of a number of metropolitan Christian communities of the Latin rite—each with its own leader or 'pope'—to being that Church to which other Latin churches would look for guidance about ecclesial policy-making, theological nuances, and liturgical practices. This last area, Christian worship, is the subject of the address in the early fifth-century missive written by Pope Innocent I, and this commentary will consider how this epistle on the historical cusp between late antiquity and the Middle Ages sheds light on areas that we continue to debate even now, over a millennium and a half later. In particular, this study seeks to highlight the relationship between Church and worship, as the title indicates.

In addition to Innocent's relatively early place in verifiable Roman church history, he is one of the earliest bishops of Rome about whom we know something concerning his role as a pastoral and theological leader. His personal and ecclesial presence is secured by the record of his correspondence. Moreover, the correspondence of others to and about Innocent furthers the historical record of the Church of Rome in this nascent period.

Except that he might have been the son of an earlier pope, there is little known of Innocent's life before his election to the episcopate of Rome. A letter of Jerome—translator, at the request of Pope Damasus, Innocent's predecessor, of the Bible from Hebrew and Greek language into Latin—suggests that Innocent was the son of the bishop Anastasius of Rome (see Jerome's Letter 130, 16). It is thought that the son, Innocent, might have served in the office of deacon during the Roman episcopate of his father, Anastasius (399-401). This is the first of such father-son papal relations, the later ones perhaps not commending this as a healthy a circumstance for the Church as this first one seems to have been. Anastasius and Innocent are buried in the same cemetery along the *via Portuensis*.[3] Innocent's papacy was relatively long and carried the Roman Church through a difficult time socially, politically, militarily, ecclesially, and theologically. He was the Bishop of Rome from 22 December 401 to 12 March 417.[4]

3   J.N.D. Kelly, *The Oxford Dictionary of Popes* (Oxford UP, 1986) pp 37-38.
4   Richard McBrien, *Lives of the Popes: The Pontiffs from St. Peter to John Paul II* pp 66f.

A. Pope Innocent I

Although Innocent's contribution to the shaping of the early medieval papacy is seminal, appreciation of his legacy is usually overshadowed by its temporal proximity to the more widely known Roman episcopates of Leo the Great (Leo I) and Gregory the Great (Gregory I). In fact it is usually the span between Leo and Gregory that is considered the transitional phase between what historians call the 'early church,' which is the time before Leo, and the 'Middle Ages,' which starts following the papacy of Gregory. The span of Leo's papacy is from 441 to 460; Gregory's from 590 to 604. In such an account, Innocent is close to the end of the early period, yet his contributions clearly lend themselves to the solidification and rise of the office of the Bishop of Rome in the Latin Church and in the Roman Empire through the Middle Ages. His oversight of the Church was already bearing the marks of the papacy whose origins are often attributed only to these later two 'greats' (*magni*), popes, and teachers of the Church.

The implications for the Church of the move from 'Bishop of Rome' to 'pope' raise ecclesial issues too complex to be dealt with fully here.[5] But the letter of this investigation has a great measure of the rhetoric of the early transition of this ecclesial office from a local and metropolitan jurisdiction to its later universal jurisdiction among the Latin rites.

About halfway through Innocent's episcopate the most politically tumultuous and ecclesially consequential event of the time took place: the conquering and pillaging of Rome by Alaric and the southward-bound barbarians at the end of the summer in the year 410. Innocent was not in the city at the time of the sacking. He had left Rome in 409 for Ravenna, the seat of the government since 404. This trip of Innocent is considered by some to be the first papal journey on behalf of the Church. In Ravenna Innocent sought to arrange a truce between the Emperor Honorius and the Gothic king Alaric, who was the leader of the migrating army that would conquer the city of Rome. Innocent's intercession, of course, was in vain, for Rome itself was soon under siege and conquered on 24 August 410, the first time in eight centuries that Rome had been so violated by foreigners. For the city and Church of Rome, the period was one of loss and liminality, tumult and transition, need and invading nemeses.

Yet, in spite of darkness emerging on the political and social horizons, the *rhetoric* of the leader of the Church in Rome was growing in strength and stridency, a key hermeneutic to keep in mind as we consider his letter on Roman worship in the early fifth century. Innocent's personal gifts and ecclesial vision, evident in his letters, shaped the relationship between government and Church that enabled the Christian faith to endure and flourish into the Middle Ages, even as virtually all other aspects of life in the Latin part of the Roman Empire were changed dramatically. As we anticipate a close look at the liturgical prescriptions from Innocent's hand, it is necessary to keep the insecurities of

---

5   For a more detailed understanding of this fifth- to seventh-century shift in the nature of the office of the Bishop of Rome, see McBrien, 73-126.

the Church context in mind. The letter's unwaveringly strong rhetoric about the liturgy and its ministers in a context of political and ecclesial uncertainty suggests a relationship between the pastoral life of churches and the prescriptions about worship that can perhaps suggest a method for the critical study of the relationship of Church and worship in other periods, such as in the sixteenth-century start of the Reformation and the Roman Catholic response at the Council of Trent, or of the late nineteenth-century loss of the papal states and the definition of papal infallibility, or of the reform of the liturgy in our own time and the initiatives to turn back some of the liturgical reforms.

B. The Episcopate in Rome before Pope Innocent I

Although Paul's Letter to the Romans does not refer to a bishop as the leader of the community, there are numerous parts of the missive that reveal conflicts (see, e.g., 16.17) that call for Paul's mediation in the community in the middle of the first century. Even his own appeals to authority—as an 'apostle' (1.1, 5)—lend weight to his giving advice about strife in the Church of Rome, particularly regarding the incorporation of Gentiles into the formerly all-Jewish Christian community. Contention characterized the Church of Rome from its birth. The conflict between those who wanted the Gentiles to become Jews by the rite of circumcision and those who sought to admit the Gentiles without such a requirement was a fundamental cleft in the community at the mid-first century (Galatians 2.1-10; Acts 15.1-29). Paul's appeals to the authority of various ministries and orders in the Church at Rome demonstrate that in a time of conflict an appeal to the authority and office of the ministers was weighed in toward the resolution of the difficulties.

So, too, in the late second century was the authority of the Church of Rome and its bishop proved ecclesially influential in the conflict about the date of Easter, or at least about it as the narrative of the conflict is recorded in Eusebius' *History of the Church*.[6] Chronicling the conflict between two traditions of paschal dating, in the East and in Rome, Eusebius wrote:

> 'Victor, head of the Roman Church, attempted at one stroke to cut off from the common unity all the Asian dioceses, together with the neighbouring churches, on the ground of heterodoxy, and pilloried them in letters in which he announced the total excommunication of all his fellow-Christians there.'[7]

Moreover, in his account of this paschal controversy, Eusebius quotes from exchanges of letters between the Greek churches and the Latin churches,

---

6   One can bear in mind, when considering the witness of Eusebius (c. 260-340) regarding the Church of Rome, that he was more than a little deferential to the office of bishop (he was himself Bishop of Caesarea), in particular to the Western see of Rome, and even to the emperor Constantine, his contemporary. *The History of the Church* includes a list of the bishops of Rome to establish its ecclesial pedigree, a surprising insertion in the chronology because he was himself the Bishop of a large church in the Greek-speaking East. See also Karl Gerlach, *The Antenicene Pascha* (Peeters, Leuven, 1998).

7   Eusebius of Caesarea, *The History of the Church*, Book 5, section 24 (trans. G.A. Williamson, Penguin, New York, 1965) pp 229-234.

thereby extending the authority of the Bishop of Rome back into a period one century before his writing of the *History*. It is likely that Eusebius's history was informed by both the ecclesial prominence of Rome and its bishop in matters such as church discipline and the deference of Eusebius to Roman ecclesial authority.

C. The Church of Rome during Innocent's Episcopate

There is, then, a range of precedents before the span of Innocent's leadership for appealing to Roman authority in times of instability and crisis elsewhere in the Church. Such a state of instability on the eve of the Empire's fall sets a context for Innocent's letter to his fellow bishop Decentius, coming as it does just a few years after the sacking of Rome and a half-century or so before the collapse of the Empire generally. Keeping this context, political and ecclesial, in mind as we read the opening paragraphs of the letter is imperative, for the ecclesiology of Innocent's appeals for uniformity in the liturgy will be heavily operative in his recommendations regarding order and ministry in the execution of the rites. This time of ecclesial vulnerability is contemporaneous with the heavy prescriptions for uniform liturgy and for exactly defined roles of ministers in worship.

We can also recall that Innocent's episcopate in Rome began shortly after the start of and ended a decade before the end of Augustine's episcopate in Hippo, North Africa. Indeed some letters were exchanged directly between the two of them during the Pelagian debates near the end of both their lives. One of Augustine's greatest and most influential works is *The City of God*, a protracted, brilliant reflection on the history of the city of Rome and its reflection on the eternal city, heaven, the City of God. While the work was not directly an apologetic explanation of how the Eternal City could have been sacked by migrating invaders and still be the centre of the Church of this world, much of Augustine's reflection emerged out of this enigma: How could the city of the Church's centre have suffered such an ignominious fate and still be the instrument of the presence of God in the world? The desperate state of the city and the Church in the period is cast not only into Augustine's stunning ecclesiology but into the correspondence from the hand of Pope Innocent I, with whom Augustine exchanged theological ideas.

The temporal overlap of the episcopates of Innocent in Rome and Augustine in Hippo (North Africa) helps us understand too their common engagement with the major theological battles of the early fifth century. Innocent, like his North African fellow bishop, was engaged in the theological battles with the Pelagians, as well as with issues similar to those, like the validity of baptisms administered by heretics, of Augustine in his battles with the Donatists. In fact, the common Latin phrase about Roman Church authority, *Roma locuta causa finita est*—'Rome has spoken, case closed'—is a paraphrase of a sentiment from Augustine about Innocent's settling of the theological issues related to the Pelagian heresy in North Africa.

7

1. Innocent's Relations with the Churches of the East

For better or worse, Innocent intervened in the administration of churches in the eastern, Greek-speaking part of the Empire. Most geographically proximate was Innocent's care and interest in the administration of the churches of Illyricum, which had earlier been in the hands of bishops like Palladius of Ratiaria and Secundianus of Singidunum, who were condemned as Arian at the council of Aquileia in Northern Italy in September 381. Also, when the source of canonical jurisdiction over the Church of Illyricum was being debated, and the metropolitans of both Constantinople and Rome sought this authority, Innocent appealed to the tradition of the authority of the Church of Rome in his own wrestling for control over that region.

Still further east, Innocent repeatedly defended John Chrysostom when the latter had been deposed from the episcopate of Constantinople and sent into exile in 404. The Roman Bishop went still further and excommunicated those who had sent Chrysostom into exile, a presentiment of the centuries-long antipathy between the Church of Rome and many of the Eastern communions. One begins to find the fissure between East and West that would continue to widen over the coming centuries. Innocent sought to call an ecumenical council to settle the matter of Chrysostom's deposition, yet, when his call went unheeded by the churches of Antioch, in West Syria, and Alexandria, in Egypt, Innocent withdrew communion from those sees. Innocent restored communion with the Church of Antioch before the end of his life, but did so only on the condition of its recognition of the ecclesiastical primacy of the Church of Rome.[8]

Finally, regarding Bethlehem, when a few of Jerome's monasteries and convents were sacked by invaders, Innocent promised the curmudgeonly scholar and translator of scripture that the authority of the Church of Rome would set about finding those responsible for the transgression and larceny. And, with another gesture of foreshadowing, he chastised John the Bishop of Jerusalem for allowing the attacks in Bethlehem to take place.

2. Innocent's Relations with Other Western Churches

Innocent was not shy about asserting the Roman office as the defender of orthodoxy on matters liturgical, biblical, theological, and ecclesiological. The evidence of Roman hubris and hegemony are manifest through his letters and it is especially evident in the introductory sentences of his letter to Bishop Decentius of Gubbio. Although it is clear that Innocent's insistence on Roman primacy might have seemed a necessary means toward the symbolic unity of the members of the Christian faith, it is not clear why he considered a communion of the apostolic sees impossible without his own, Rome, outranking the others. Yet, in responding to the African bishops who sought his direction in their strife with the Pelagians, Innocent proclaimed near the end of this life, 'All ecclesiastical matters throughout the world are, by divine right, to be referred to the apostolic see, that is, to Peter, the author of its name and honour.' Again, *Roma locuta causa finita est*, 'case closed.'

---

8   See Ep. 24.

3. The Letters of Innocent

Innocent's efforts and influence are chronicled in the progress of the extant correspondence, thirty-six letters in all.[9] In the theological realm, Innocent's episcopate followed the earlier two Christological councils of the early church— Nicea (3) and of Constantinople (381)—while it just antedated the latter two— Ephesus (431) and Chalcedon (451).

Innocent's theological and political discernment was key in having the Roman Church navigate its way through some of the christologically controversial and tenuous issues of the day. We find, for example, correspondence from Innocent that bears on the Pelagian controversy of North Africa regarding human nature and humanity's capacity to participate in the life of God after baptism, issues about which we know most from the life and writings of Augustine of Hippo, to whom some of Innocent's letters are addressed.

The letters are the only extant works from this Bishop of Rome, and there is no indication from the letters that there were other works from his hand. Though he was a very engaged participant in the theological disputes in the Latin Church, there are no theological tracts separate from what he had written in the letters. He also wrote to councils of bishops gathered in Spain to address order in their churches, and therein he addresses how they might deal with the Arian heresy in Toledo; about the theology of the catholic bishops against Pelagian heresy in Carthage, North Africa, an exchange that he participates in until the very end of his life.

In addition to the theological issues taken up when addressing councils of bishops gathering to discuss heretics at their doors seeking admission, Innocent dealt at great length with the discipline and order of the Church's ministers and ministrations. He wrote that the *baptisms* of former heretics are to be recognized as valid only if the heretical churches had used water and the Trinitarian formula for the rites, but advocates that no *ordinations* of former heretics be so recognized; that bishops cannot make other bishops outside of their metropolitan sphere (Letter 2.1); that, even after penance and reconciliation, members of the military cannot be admitted to the ranks of the clergy; that anyone who, whether before or after baptism, has taken a widow as a spouse, cannot seek to be a member of the clergy, though men who have married virgins are still eligible for ordination; that one church cannot steal a cleric from another church; that a committed virgin who later marries cannot be admitted for penance. He wrote about the changing marital status of catechumens and those elected for baptism; about those who become widows and widowers before and after baptism; and about the reconciliation of clerics who formerly belonged to heretical churches or sects.

---

9   The letter that is the subject of this study is number of the thirty-eight extant missives. The collection of the letters of Innocent is available in J.-P. Migne, *Patrologia Latina* 20: 463-608 (Coustant, 1721); Migne, *Patrologia Latina* 84:657f (Gonzales, 1821). The source of the Latin text of this work comes from the critical edition in Robert Cabié, *La lettre du pape Innocent I a Decentius de Gubbio (19 Mars 416): Texte critique, traduction et commentaire* (Publications Universitaires de Louvain, Louvain, 1973).

Moreover, he wrote that eunuchs—'those who have amputated part of their bodies,' *partem sibi corporis amputavit*—cannot become members of the clergy; that bigamists cannot become members of the clergy; that those with concubines cannot be admitted to the clergy. Here we also find references to both clerical marriage and clerical celibacy; to what books of scripture were considered canonical and what books, though read in the assembly, were not canonical (Letter 6). He excluded a few of the books that eventually become canonical for Roman Catholics, but these are among those not included in the Jewish and Protestant canons of the Hebrew Bible. He also wrote about how to celebrate the rites of the church properly; how the different dates of Easter in different communions broke up the unity of the Church; how the practices of the Church of Rome were to be held up as the model for the other churches in communion with Rome, particularly in Illyricum, in Spain, France, and elsewhere in Italy.

Although today ecumenical issues most often revolve around the celebration of the Eucharist, it is clear that in Innocent's time the issues of unity and excommunication were discussed regarding the admission to and celebration of *baptism*. While this may reveal differences in the sacramental significance of these rites, it is also likely a result of the fact that most initiated today are infants while in Innocent's time most initiated would have been adults.

Even though the invasion of the city of Rome by Alaric and his troops happened in the middle of Innocent's 16-year episcopate in the Church there, one finds little in the letters that reveal the drama of such a catastrophe. Undeterred by this secular threat, Innocent wrote confidently about the Petrine privilege of the Roman episcopate, drawing on the Gospel of Matthew for the text that, since the fifth century, has been employed as the proof-text for the primacy of the Bishop of Rome in the Roman Catholic ecclesiology:

'And Jesus answered him, "Blessed are you, Simon son of Jonah! For flesh and blood has not revealed this to you, but my Father in heaven. And I tell you, you are Peter, and on this rock I will build my church, and the gates of Hades will not prevail against it. I will give you the keys of the kingdom of heaven, and whatever you bind on earth will be bound in heaven, and whatever you loose on earth will be loosed in heaven".' (16.17-19, NRSV)

Innocent was the very first to make this ecclesiological link between the apostle Peter and the Bishop of Rome, a link that has been maintained by Roman Catholic ecclesiology and theology for over a millennium and a half.

The barbarian threat from the outside might have contributed to Innocent's efforts to tighten up the behaviour of the clergy and to circumscribe liturgical norms. Frequently he strives for 'the complete rigour of ecclesiastical authority' (Letter 1) and appeals to the precedent of his authority founded in the apostle Peter. As he describes it in Letter 2, he asks for 'the help of the holy apostle Peter, on which this apostolate and episcopate has been founded by Christ from the start,' and he makes a case for the purity and blamelessness of this office based on Paul, so that he might 'present the church [to Christ] in splendour, without a spot or wrinkle or anything of the kind—yes, so that she may be holy and without blemish' (Ephesians 5.27). This purity and splendour, by Innocent's reckoning, will be maintained by the stability of 'our traditions, handed on by word and by letter' (2 Thessalonians 2.14).

4. Letter 25

The letter of this study, translation, and investigation is unique in a number of ways. It is among the very earliest of witnesses to liturgical practice in the Church of Rome. Though readers may be surprised that a *fifth*-century text is among the earliest witnesses to the rites of the Church of Rome, the extant evidence about Roman worship in the first four centuries is scant. For this reason the letter has received much attention from historians of the Roman Church and its liturgy.

Moreover, some of the topics taken up in the letter are still quite contended in Christian liturgical life now a millennium and a half later, and so again the witness of an 'early' community in the city of Rome lends an important testimony to the contribution of tradition. Such liturgical matters taken up by Innocent that are still debated now sixteen centuries later are the anointing of infants, the reservation of the Eucharist for distribution to the sick, the rites of exorcism, the place of the sign of peace in the Eucharistic liturgy, the place of petitions in the Eucharistic prayer, the anointing of the sick, the rite of reconciliation of penitents, as well as the tradition of the Saturday fast.

Scholarship has also attended to the nature of episcopal authority in the Church during Innocent's time and to how Innocent's view of his role in the 'universal' Church contributed to the eventual emergence of the office of the pope. Unfortunately, the studies that take up the issues of authority and ecclesiology in Innocent's letter rarely, if ever, address the connection between the letter's ecclesiological stance and its liturgical recommendations. In addition to commenting on the liturgy, the most significant newness herein links Roman worship in the early fifth century with the state of the Church of the time. Up to now, studies have either considered particular liturgical matters apart from the letter as a whole or apart from the ecclesiology of the letter, or they have focused on the contribution of Innocent in establishing the papacy, but done so without tying this to Innocent's dictates about liturgical uniformity. This study considers the liturgical recommendations as a means for Innocent to have established ecclesial authority for himself and the bishops to succeed him.

D. The Church of Gubbio

While we have thirty-eight letters from Innocent, we know virtually nothing about the one to whom this particular Roman missive was sent, Decentius, the Bishop of the small see of Gubbio.[10] The little we do know about the Umbrian bishop and his church community are drawn almost exclusively from close readings of the material in Innocent's letter, for we have neither other contemporary evidence from the area nor the initial letter of inquiry Decentius

---

10   The Latin name for Gubbio, as used by Innocent in the address of the letter, is Egubium.

had addressed to Innocent's predecessor in Rome, Pope Damasus.[11] Since Damasus died before he had responded to Decentius, the task fell to Innocent. How did it come to pass that this relatively insignificant worshipping community in Gubbio had so many questions about the liturgy for which its own bishop sought direction from the Bishop of Rome? Would not the Church of Rome have had such supreme liturgical authority at the time that its influence would have been immediately felt and followed?

1. Gubbio: At the Crossroads of Four Metropolitan Churches
Liturgical and ecclesiological studies of this period of the Christian faith remind us that *Rome* was not the only centre of theology and rites. On the Italian peninsula alone there were other churches with as great—and, at times, perhaps greater— a liturgical, theological, and ecclesial prominence. In addition to the Church of Rome—whose fourth- and fifth-century authority was manifested in the increasing influence accorded its Bishop—there were three other metropolitan churches as close to Gubbio geographically as the Church of Rome. These were the metropolitan churches of *Milan*, *Aquileia*, and *Ravenna*, and in the early period of Christianity the bishops of those churches had at least as much ecclesial authority in their metropolitan areas as had the Bishop of Rome over his metropolitan area. Perhaps to our surprise, we have a greater bounty of liturgical remnants in the early period from leaders of these three major churches than we have from the Church and leaders in Rome, and we are surer of their influence than we are about the practices of the Church of Rome in the same period. Near Gubbio would have been the churches of Milan, Ravenna, and Aquileia, strong seats of ecclesial and governmental and military influence, to which we turn.

a. The Metropolitan Church of Milan and its Bishop Ambrose
The figure of history from Milan about whom we know the most is the eminent Bishop Ambrose, who was the leader of this major see from 374 until 397, just a few years before Innocent became his father's successor as the Bishop of Rome.[12] Ambrose's ecclesial and political patrimony cannot be overestimated, for his influence with the emperor during the Arian crisis of 381 has been critically demonstrated.[13] But even more so can we learn about the liturgy of late fourth-century Milan from the writing of Ambrose.

As the son of a government minister over the prefecture of Gaul, Ambrose was born in Trier—in western Germany now, not far east of Luxemburg—

---

11 The death of Damasus in 401 led to the election of a new Bishop in Rome, and thus to the letter of response coming not from the one addressed but from his successor.

12 For a fuller treatment of the life of Ambrose, see J.R. Palanque, *Saint Ambroise et l'Empire Romain. Contribution à l'histoire des rapports de l'Église et de'État à fin du quatrième siécle* (E. de Boccard, Paris, 1933); Frederick Homes Dudden, *Saint Ambrose: His Life and Times* I and II (Clarendon, Oxford, 1935); Angelo Paredi, *S. Ambrogio e la sua età* (Hoepli, Milan, 1960).

13 Neil McLynn, *Ambrose of Milan: Church and Court in a Christian Capital* (University of California Press, Berkeley, 1994); and Daniel H. Williams, *Ambrose of Milan and the End of the Nicene-Arian Conflicts* (Clarendon, Oxford, 1995).

and had himself lived in Rome, though unbaptized at that time. His sister Marcellina was a consecrated virgin in Rome and the future Bishop of Milan was at her veiling and, in spite of not being initiated, Ambrose demonstrated familiarity with Christian theology and practices of the Church of Rome. Once he was Bishop, he became closely allied with the emperor Gratian, whose support he gained in the strife over Arianism.

Ambrose was apologetic, it seems from some of his writings, about the ways in which the liturgical practices of the Church of Milan diverged from the practices of the Church of Rome. Indeed about the foot-washing element in the rites of initiation, Ambrose wrote:

'We know that the Roman Church, *whose example and form we follow in all things*, does not have this custom. Yet the Roman Church does not have this rite of washing the feet perhaps because of the great number of people there. But some try to excuse themselves from it by explaining that it should be done as a mystery, not as baptism not as regeneration, or that the washing of the feet should be done as a host does for guests.'[14]

Perhaps Ambrose was trying to justify the practice because it was so deeply embedded in the Milanese liturgical tradition that he could not entertain the possibility of not presiding over this rite with its remnants of initiatory meaning.[15] Yet Ambrose sought to have his own metropolitan Church be like the Church of Rome in all things.

There are other liturgical elements in which the Milanese practice diverged from that of Rome, but one senses in Ambrose's deference to Rome not only his desire to conform, but also the emerging authority of the Bishop of Rome as had not earlier been the situation. When we look at Innocent's ecclesiological presumptions at the beginning of the letter to Decentius, we will see that he begins to cast the Church of Rome in a role of primacy as had not been done by his predecessors in the episcopate there.

b. The Exarchate of Aquileia and its Bishop Chromatius

Still another metropolitan Church of influence in the region was Aquileia, situated on the Adriatic just to the west of present-day Croatia. The Church of Aquileia was at approximately the same distance from Gubbio as was the Church of Milan, but, different from Milan, the influence of the Aquileian Christian community was curbed considerably in the fifth and sixth centuries as a result of the destruction at the hands of the barbarian invaders. Yet travellers from Aquileia to Rome would have passed through Gubbio, and this was still another influence on the worship in the community of Decentius.

The uniqueness of the metropolitan Church of Aquileia has been more prominent in recent decades as a result of the deeper patrimony of the community of Aquileia recognizable since the attribution of sermons and

14 *De sacramentis* III, 5; my translation.
15 See Pier Franco Beatrice, *La lavanda dei piedi: Contributo alla storia delle antiche liturgie christiane* (CLV-Edizioni Liturgiche, Rome, 1983).

tracts to its Bishop Chromatius.[16] Until recently the only extant writings or exhortations from Chromatius were 18 tracts on the Gospel of Matthew, a sermon on the beatitudes, and a short preface on the Our Father.[17] In quantity and in liturgical and theological contribution, especially, the corpus of Chromatius's work has widened our view of the unique liturgical practices of this metropolitan see considerably. Aquileia had a fervently active port on the Adriatic, thereby giving it open access to the culture and church customs of the Eastern parts of the Empire, as well as to Africa and Spain. Jerome lived in Chromatius's community from 370 to 373, before he left for the East, and Rufinus, the translator of some of the works of Origen into Latin, was baptized at Aquileia in 370.

Because it did not fare well as a city or a church after the beginning of the Middle Ages, the Church of Aquileia did not leave as many traces of its unique liturgical practices as did Ambrose's Church of Milan. Nevertheless, we know of its introduction of the Apostle's Creed into the liturgy, its unique insertion of the narrative of the Christ's descent to the dead into the Easter vigil, and, like Milan, Aquileia was among those churches that had likely at one time initiated new Christians by washing feet.[18] Perhaps with still other unique worship elements, the traditions of the Church of Aquileia would also have come to Gubbio by way of travelling Christians on their way to Rome from the Adriatic port-city of Aquileia.

c. The Metropolitan Church of Ravenna and its Bishop Peter Chrysologus
In its struggles between Arians and Nicenes as well as in its unique liturgical practices and configuration of the church year, the Church of Ravenna was likely also to have been a bearer on the concerns of Decentius of Gubbio about the correct way of celebrating the rites of the Church. On the northeastern shore of the Italian peninsula, Ravenna, like Aquileia, would have had commercial and cultural exposure to the world of the eastern Mediterranean Sea, including churches such as Antioch, Jerusalem, and Alexandria. The largest bounty of evidence from this Church comes in the many extant sermons from the episcopate of its Bishop Peter Chrysologus, who was the leader of this Church in the second quarter of the fifth century, beginning, most likely, just a few years after the death of Innocent, in 417.[19]

Moreover, any fifth-century Christian travelling between Ravenna, the seat of the imperial government, and Rome, as it became increasingly the

---

16 *Chromatii Aquileiensis Opera*, ed. R. Ètaix and J. Lemarié, CCSL 9a (Brepols, Turnholt, 1974); *Spicilegium ad Chromatii Aquileiensis opera, Supplementum* (Brepols, Turnholt, 1977); *Sermons* I and II, ed. Joseph Lemarié, French trans. Henri Tardif, SC 154 and 164 (Cerf, Paris, 1969 and 1971).
17 See *Chromatii Aquileinsis episcopi quae supersunt*, ed. A. Hoste, CCSL 9 (Brepols, Turnholt, 1957) pp 371-447.
18 See Beatrice, as above: pages 85-91.
19 See especially the exacting study of Franco Sottocornola, *L'anno liturgico dei sermoni di Pietro Crisologo: Ricerca storico-critica sulla liturgia di Ravenna antica* (Centro Studi e Ricerche sulla Antica Provincia Ecclesiastica Ravennata, Cesena, 1973).

centre of church authority, would have passed through Gubbio. This would be so even of those from Coptic, Greek, and Syrian cultures, who, before moving southwestward to Rome, would have disembarked on the shore of Ravenna. The Christians of Gubbio, therefore, would have heard about liturgical traditions different from their own from such travellers who visited and celebrated the liturgy with the community at Ravenna. For Gubbio, then and today, is 'found right at the halfway point between Rome and Ravenna, near the Via Flammina that connects the Flamina region with Rome.'[20]

The influences of these churches, then, on the much smaller community of worshippers in Gubbio would have been greater than on a church outside of the Northern Italian cluster of metropolitan churches. A key issue in the ecclesial sphere of both Ravenna and Gubbio would have been about determining the degree of liturgical diversity one might sustain among churches that were ecclesially and theologically one. Perhaps a greater spectrum of liturgical diversity was more tolerable in the more peaceful span before the invasions from the north, from the early fourth century to the early fifth. Yet the letter of Innocent to Decentius signals the concern of the Bishop of Rome that uniformity in worship traditions is connected to uniformity in theology and ecclesiology.

Northern Italy, with its cluster of both metropolitan churches on the grand scale of Milan and Ravenna, as well as the many lesser cathedral communities, such as those of Chromatius of Aquileia and of poor old Decentius—with his inquiries addressed in the lost letter to Damasus of Rome—would have been a prime area for establishing the degree of unity and diversity permissible in the Christian Church—theologically, ecclesiologically, and liturgically.

Knowing that Gubbio is so positioned near these three metropolitans helps us appreciate some of the weight from and practical bearing on the Bishop who wrote to Innocent's predecessor for ecclesial and liturgical advice and support. It seems likely that some of the worshippers in Decentius's community had come to him asking, 'Why is it that we hear about celebrating the liturgy *this* way in Rome and *that* way in Ravenna?,' about '*this* way in Ravenna and *that* way in Aquileia?' or '*This* way in Aquileia and *that* way in Milan?' or '*This* way in Milan and *that* way in Rome?' 'Why don't we do this?,' one can hear a worshipper asking as we read Innocent's prescriptions. And maybe Decentius found himself stumped as he tried to discern what practices and what authority to heed. Fortunately for us, he sat down to address his concerns to the Bishop of Rome, whose authority was ascending in the early fifth century.

In history the Church of Gubbio is mentioned perhaps most often in relation to a famous thirteenth-century character, Saint Francis of Assisi, whose autobiography has the well-known story about the 'wolf of Gubbio.' Gubbio was not a large place, nor was it of much consequence when its Bishop sought the liturgical counsel of

---

20   Sottocornola, page 30; my translation of the original.

the Bishop of Rome. That Decentius, about whom we know virtually nothing except what is ascertained from this letter, is the Church's second most famous character—second, that is, to the wolf—is both accurate and telling.

The birthplace of Francis, in Assisi, is not far from Gubbio, about one hundred miles north of Rome. The town's Church would have been found along one's travelling route between the city of Rome and the some of the largest cities and churches of Northern Italy. In the first millennium, before the birth of Francis, Milan, Aquileia, and Ravenna would have been destinations for tourists and for important people who had dealings in matters of the military, government, or church in the span of the episcopates of Innocent in Rome and Decentius in Gubbio. Situated along a major travelling route, the town and Church of Gubbio would have been under the influence of these major liturgical centres. The Church of Gubbio might have found questions emerging as it discovered the different liturgical practices of different communities of faith at the end of late antiquity and the beginning of the Middle Ages.

E. The Roman Empire and the Roman Church

The letter from Innocent of Rome to Decentius of Northern Italy has not been ignored or forgotten completely since its composition over a millennium and a half ago. But for the most part, attention to the letter has usually been drawn either because it is among the earliest witnesses to the episcopal teaching authority of the Bishop of Rome[21] or because of its revelations about a particular liturgical topic about which Decentius inquired or to which Innocent responded. The letter is most frequently highlighted today in histories of a particular liturgical custom, but seeing these customs in the ecclesial context of the early fifth century and the invasions from the north is necessary.

We have mentioned that earlier scholarship has tended to write of the letter either when tracing the history of papal authority or when tracing the history of a particular liturgical custom. What has been missed is what would relate the former to the latter: indeed, what was it about the office of the Bishop of Rome in the early fifth century which supplied the authority about liturgical customs? Moreover, how did the Bishop of Rome balance his ecclesial office with theological interventions during the Christological crises of his episcopate? Further, what was the relationship between the authority of the Roman Bishop on Christological matters and his authority on liturgical practices? Finally, how were the changes in theology and Christology related to the Bishop's advocacy for particular liturgical practices?

---

21 Much of the scholarship regarding the teaching authority of the Bishop of Rome and the role of the Roman Bishop in the implementing of liturgical practices comes from nineteenth-century German liturgical scholarship. Others have noted the ominous precedent such scholarship has, in retrospect, when we see the kind of straitening of life and practices and populations attempted in Germany in the twentieth century.

While this letter been raised in research and discussions about the origins of the office of the papacy or about the anointing at baptism, the sign of peace at the Eucharist, praying the intercessions, about bringing communion to the sick, and so on, attention has not mined it for how the office of the Bishop of Rome would have related to the particular liturgical prescriptions. This study seeks to link these two spheres.

It is beneficial to think about the state of the Roman Empire at the time when the letter was written as well as about how the life of the government bore upon the Church of Rome. This investigation will also consider these topics below in order to contextualize the ecclesiastical and ritual particulars of the letter, and to consider how the letter's introduction on the nature of the teaching authority of the Bishop of Rome relates to the liturgical matters raised by Decentius's inquiry and Innocent's response.

Introduction to the Letter (Four Parts)

The Latin text that follows is from the text of the letter in the critical edition by Robert Cabié.[22] An English translation will follow the Latin text; following the translation will, as needed, be a discussion of the relevant variants in the manuscript tradition or of key words and phrases; a study of the contribution of the letter to the history of the liturgy; and some consideration of the theological implications of the liturgical instruction.

Introduction, Part One

Si instituta ecclesiastica ut sunt a beatis apostolis tradita integra vellent servare Domini sacerdotes, nulla diversitas, nulla varietas in ipsis ordinibus ac consecrationibus haberetur. Sed dum unusquisque non quod traditum est, sed quod sibi visum fuerit, hoc existimat esse tenendum, inde diversa in diversis locis vel ecclesiis aut teneri aut celebrari videntur; ac fit scandalum populis, qui dum nesciunt traditiones antiquas humana praesumptione corruptas, putant sibi aut ecclesias non convenire, aut ab apostolis vel apostolicis ipsis contrarietatem inductam.

If priests of the Lord wanted to preserve those church customs in their fullness as they have been handed down from the blessed apostles, there should be no diversity, no variety in these rites and blessings. But as long as each one tries to maintain not what was handed on but what appears to have been handed on, different customs will be kept or celebrated in various places or churches; and so this stirs up scandal in the people, who—ignorant of the ancient traditions, now corrupted by human presumption—think that the churches themselves do not agree or are led to practices contrary to those coming from the apostles.

Textual variants: While one can find manuscripts in which the greatest number of variants at the beginning of a text, as the scribe might have adapted the text for the new context in which the words would have been read or spoken, here in the introductory matters of this letter of Pope Innocent the variants are relatively few. Perhaps the gravity of the ecclesiological issues taken up to establish the authority of the Church of Rome and the authority of the Bishop of Rome secured the integrity of the text into the Middle Ages when it was copied. The gravity might have curbed any inclinations toward variants, yet there are a few worth noting.

Two manuscripts from the same textual lineage add the Latin *papa*, meaning 'pope,' into the title of the letter, indicating, if slightly at this point, the emerging authority that the Bishop of Rome would gain in succeeding centuries. Both are manuscripts in Munich, with the older one coming from the late eighth or early ninth centuries.

22   See note 11 above.

Also, two manuscripts of the same lineage omit the word 'not' from the sentence relating that the scandalized people would think that 'the churches themselves do agree' instead of 'do not agree.'

Key words: The phrase *instituta ecclesiastica*, 'church customs,' is unique when Innocent uses it in this letter. It has no precedents in the Latin literature of Christianity up to the time of this letter. The emergence of this kind of vocabulary from the Bishop of Rome is yet another indication of the changing role of the Church of Rome in the Latin tradition and of the straitening of liturgical and ecclesial customs so that they are rooted in the Roman liturgy.

History: The context of the city of Rome at the time when the letter was written is very important in understanding the opening of the letter. As a sign of the Church and of the Church's stability, the Bishop of Rome needs to communicate security and immobility, particularly when the situation is in flux. The time of Innocent's letter is a time of incomparable instability, as it comes after the conquest of the city of Rome and before the fall of the Roman Empire completely about a half-century later. The northerners invaded the city while Innocent himself was up in Ravenna trying to plead for a negotiation between the emperor and the Visigothic leader. Innocent returns to the occupied city, and the letter reflects his efforts at stabilizing the Church as the world in which it lived is falling down around it. Recognizing the social and political upheavals of Rome in the time of Innocent's letter is key in understanding the exigencies in which the liturgical prescriptions to follow are mandated.

Theology: A presumption of the author here is that there is only one way to do the rites. In this assertion he is erasing, by ignorance or by calculation, the diversity of ritual traditions that are evident in the gospels themselves. The stability of the Church is being rendered as dependent on liturgical uniformity, and this is a relatively new ecclesiological and liturgical idea. The effort of Innocent's rule in the context of the falling of the empire suggests a possible hermeneutic of heavy liturgical prescriptions in a time when the church is changing. The leader of the church in this time of instability moves him to legislate holding on to what is familiar and claiming as apostolic one's own liturgical practice.

Introduction, Part Two

Quis enim nesciant aut non advertat id quod a principe apostolorum Petro Romanae ecclesiae traditum est, ac nunc usque custoditur ab omnibus debere servari nec superduci aut introduci aliquid quod aut auctoritatem non habeat, aut aliunde accipere videatur exemplum, praesertim cum sit manifestum in omnem Italiam, Gallias, Spanias, Africam itaque Siciliam et insulas interiacentes nullum instituisse ecclesias, nisi eos quos venerabilis apostolus Petrus aut eius successores constituerint sacerdotes. Aut legant si in his provinciis alius apostolorum invenitur aut legitur docuisse.

For who does not know or who is not aware of what has been handed down to the Church of Rome from the prince of the apostles, Peter, or that this has been guarded and followed by all until now? Nothing without authority is to be displace or be introduced, nor should something from another place be considered a model. Unless these have been introduced by the esteemed apostle Peter or his priest-successors, nothing is to be introduced into churches in all of Italy, in Gaul, Spain, Africa and Sicily and the nearby islands. Let them read and find out if another apostle is found to have been in those parts or if he is found to have taught there.

Textual variants: Most of the variants here are in the spelling of the place names according to local usage. A seventh-century manuscript does omit the name Peter, leaving the question about the handing on of the rites by the 'prince of the apostles,' but not having Peter as the historical or scriptural referent.

Key words: The geography of Innocent's concerns is worth highlighting. In the introduction we saw the importance of the metropolitan churches of Ravenna, Milan, and Aquileia, yet here Innocent is claiming liturgical authority for 'all of Italy,' and then his authoritative reach extends to 'Gaul, Spain, Africa, Sicily, and the nearby islands.' These are all within the Latin tradition of the fifth century, but covering a wide swathe of Christianity.

Sacerdotes could have indicated 'priests' or 'bishops,' for in this period there is testimony to both as the meaning of this word. In using 'priest-successors' I distinguish this from *presbyter* which is a Latin word from a Greek word with origins in the New Testament with some basis for ministry.

History and Theology: The immutability of the rites as a sign of the church is important in this section. Refiguring what we know to be untrue, Innocent suggests that there had been liturgical uniformity, one way of celebrating, from the time of Peter until his time. Liturgical history suggests the opposite to have been true.

The last sentence of this section seems to suggest that apostolic authority might have led to some liturgical variety if the church had been founded by an apostle other than Peter. This is slightly different from what the earlier part describes, as if all churches had been following the same liturgical prescriptions from the apostolic. This qualification opens up the possibility that Innocent knew that some churches had been founded by different apostles and that some liturgical variety would have followed upon the different apostolic foundations. Nevertheless, Innocent is clearly mandating that nothing new is to be added to the current liturgical practice.

Introduction, Part Three

Qui si non legunt, quia nusquam inveniunt, oportet eos hoc sequi, quod ecclesia Romana custodit a qua eos principium accepisse non dubium est, ne dum peregrinis assertionibus student, caput institutionum videantur omittere. Saepe dilectionem tuam ad Urbem venisse, ac nobiscum in ecclesia convenisse, non dubium est, et quem morem vel in consecrandis mysteriis, vel in caeteris agendis arcanis teneat cognovisse. Quod sufficere arbitrarer ad informationem ecclesiae tuae, vel reformationem si praecessores tui minus aliquid aut aliter tenuerunt satis certum haberem, nisi de aliquibus consulendos nos esse duxisses.

So if they do not read it (for there is nothing to be found), they should follow what is done in the Roman Church, from which—let there be no doubt—they derive their own origin. This is to be done so that, in their eagerness to track down wandering rumours, they are not seen to ignore the very source of their own foundation. We know that you have often come to our City, that you have come to Church with us, and that you have held onto the customs that you have experienced when the mysteries and the other secret rites were celebrated here. I have considered this sufficiently in the formation or reformation of your own Church—particularly if your predecessors have found something less or something else—since you have led the way in consulting us about certain issues.

Textual variants: There are few variants with consequences for the history of the liturgy within this section. Yet there is a late seventh-century manuscript from Liège which omits the 'no' from the first sentence, suggesting that 'there *is* doubt' about the rites being derived from the Roman Church.

Key words: The words *principium* and *caput* indicate that Innocent is beginning to advocate that the authority of the Church of Rome is supreme over even the authority of the local bishops. Innocent is claiming for his church the position as the 'beginning,' *principium* and as 'head,' *caput*. Indeed, Innocent tells Decentius, even if your predecessors in the diocese have done something different, you have done well in 'consulting us' as the supreme authority in matters of worship.

Theology: This ecclesiology of Innocent's letter is telling, for Innocent is striving to displace the ecclesiology that would have found Rome as one of the few centres of authority. Innocent is recommending that if there is a conflict between the custom of your predecessors and what is done in Rome, Rome is the church that should be consulted. Innocent praised Decentius's initiative in consulting the Church of Rome, perhaps signalling that this was a new tradition and one that—in his interest as its leader—the Church of Rome wanted to encourage.

Introduction, Part Four

Quibus idcirco respondemus, non quod te aliqua ignorare credamus, sed ut maiore auctoritate vel tuos instituas, vel si qui a Romanae ecclesiae institutionibus errant, aut commoneas aut indicare non differas ut scire valeamus qui sint qui aut novitates inducunt aut alterius ecclesiae quam Romanae, existimant consuetudinem esse servandam.

We are therefore responding with regard to these issues, not because we believe you to be uninformed about certain issues, but that with greater authority you might instruct those who belong to your Church. Or, if there are some who deviate from the ways established by the Roman Church, then you can warn them or tell us about them without delay so that we are able to know those who are introducing new ways or ways different from what is done in the Roman Church, so that they can try to observe our custom.

Textual Variants, Key Words: There are no consequential textual variants, key words that have not already been taken up in this introduction of Innocent's letter.

History: What is of importance here is not only the earlier mandate that Decentius and other churches follow the liturgical customs of the Roman Church, but that the Roman Church itself is soliciting information about any Church that does not observe the Roman liturgical tradition. No longer is the local bishop autonomous regarding the liturgy in his own diocese but Innocent is putting himself higher in authority over the local church than the local bishop. This is a novel ecclesiological tradition of the Roman Church and a new ecclesiology. Innocent is appealing for Decentius's help in establishing the authority in the Roman Church.

Theology: Because liturgical diversity had characterized the church's rites, at least of baptism and Eucharist, from the New Testament until the early fifth century, this mandate for uniformity and threat about the consequences of diversity is novel. Innocent seeks to eliminate the diversity that had been a key part of Christian ritual traditions from the start.

This is the end of the introductory part of Innocent's letter, yet one can see in this introduction the state of the church in this time of crisis as well as the importance of worship in the bishop's effort to stabilize his own church and the churches throughout much of the Latin tradition. As the letter moves into addressing particular liturgical customs, it is important for us to bear the ecclesial context in mind, for Innocent will again and again assert that the customs had been immobile from the beginning, from the apostle Peter and the early communities until Innocent. Yet history tells us that this was not so. Diversity in the rites was the custom from the earliest record of the New Testament until the middle of the fourth century, particularly in the Northern Italian area from which Decentius sent his missive to the bishop of Rome.

1
On the Peace

Pacem igitur asseris ante confecta mysteria quosdam populis imperare, vel sibi inter sacerdotes tradere, cum post omnia quae aperire non debeo pax sit necessario indicenda per quam constet populum ad omnia quae in mysteriis aguntur atque in ecclesia celebrantur praebuisse consensum ac finita esse pacis concludentis signaculo demonstrentur.

You mention that some demand that the peace take place, or be offered among the priests themselves, before the mysteries themselves have taken place. In fact the peace should take place after all those things about which I must not speak. The peace shows that the people have been brought together concerning what has taken place in all of the mysteries celebrated in Church. In the peace the people offer their consent and acknowledge it as the closing sign of peace.

Textual variants: In one significant version of the letter, from a ninth-century manuscript from the abbey at Fulda, in one finds the opening word *pacem* replaced by *precem*, a consequential difference suggesting that there are some who order that the 'prayer take before the mysteries themselves have taken place.' Also, a number of scribes omitted the 'not' so that his 'things about which I must not speak' become the 'things about which I must speak.'

Key words: The 'peace'—rendered here as *pacem*, the accusative case of *pax*—is what communities today would generally call the 'exchange of peace,' or 'sign of peace,' or, less frequently, unfortunately, the 'kiss of peace.'

As throughout the letter, the Latin *sacerdotes* is here translated by 'priests,' even though it may refer to the 'bishops' who would exchange the peace among themselves. There is a warrant for either 'priests' or 'bishops,' and the former is chosen because *episcopus* is used in the letter and translated as 'bishop.'

Regarding 'after all those things about which I must not speak,' one can presume that it is for mystagogical reasons that Innocent cannot speak about the things that take place during the Eucharistic liturgy. Such secrecy about the rites is familiarly called the *disciplina arcani*, leaving to the surprise of the senses of those being initiated what will actually take place during the rites of initiation. Post-baptismal catechesis will draw on the surprise of the physical, sensory experience of the rites so that the mystagogical preaching will bring the neophytes to an appreciation of the physical efficacy of the sacraments in which they have been brought into the Church.

History: The history of the 'peace' has been of some consequence in the revision of the Christian Eucharistic rite in churches over the past few decades, and Innocent's letter has been taken up as a proof-text for the peace after the Eucharistic prayer. The kiss is present from the earliest stratum of Christian literature, the letters of Paul, where it appears either as a liturgical rubric for a kiss as a ritual exchange or as a customary greeting of the genre of letter-writing in antiquity.[23] Because the Greek word for 'spirit,' *pneuma*, also bears the meaning 'breath,' this juxtaposition suggests that the kiss, consciously or not, allowed for an exchange of breath as an exchange of the Holy Spirit. The occasional use of 'holy' with both the kiss and the Spirit further confirms this suggestion. Moreover, in the Gospel of John, Jesus 'breathes' on the disciples when he gives them the holy 'spirit.'

Holding that the Holy Spirit builds up the Church, one can find here that the kiss is a means by which that upbuilding is ritualized. In second- and third-centuries texts—*Apostolic Tradition* of Rome, Tertullian and Cyprian, both of North Africa—the kiss appears in liturgical contexts, but not all Eucharistic. It concludes various aspects of rites of baptism and reconciliation. Though not Eucharistic, these rites are contributions to the task of the Holy Spirit in building up the Church. The rhetoric of some in the early period make us know that the kiss began to have disreputable erotic associations in the minds of unbelievers, and those who write of it clarify that it is a holy kiss not an erotic one.

Liturgical scholar L. Edward Phillips has rightly questioned today's sensibilities about what is claimed to be the restoration of a practice from the early church:

'Is it really equivalent to substitute another "sign" of peace for a "kiss"? We may wonder whether a handshake or even an embrace could function in the same way. While it is highly unlikely that an actual kiss on the mouth, as attested in many patristic sources, could even be re-introduced into modern practice, it is a mistake to assume that this was an easy matter for the early church. Christians defying cultural norms when they kissed each other within their communities, and this provided the basis for scandal.'[24]

Perhaps we think of this as a matter of inculturation, dismissing the possibility of a lips-to-lips kiss in the liturgy today. 'Oh, they were used to doing things that way in those places and times,' we might think. Or, 'we know more about hygiene than they did.' Maybe this is so. But, as Phillips poses the question and as we read of Innocent's recommendation, we wonder if the kissing of strangers in a Christian assembly could have been any more comfortable in the first few centuries of Christian tradition than it would be today. For they were not practising the kiss as a sign of familial love or social friendship; the ritual gesture was a commitment to demonstrating an ecclesial bond apart from those other ties.

In those days there was a disjuncture between the values of society and church, but today we have restored many of the ancient rites because the disjuncture between society and church is today much more like it was in the first half-millennium of Christian history than it was for the intervening

23   See, for example, Romans 16.16; 1 Corinthians 16.20; 2 Corinthians 13.12; and 1 Thessalonians 5.26:
      'Greet one another with a holy kiss.' There one finds the holy kiss juxtaposed to references to the
      'Spirit of Christ,' as in L. Edward Phillips, *The Ritual Kiss in Early Christian Worship* (Alcuin/GROW
      Joint Liturgical Study 36, Grove Books Limited, Cambridge, 1996) pp 9-15.
24   Phillips, *The Ritual Kiss* pp 36.

centuries. Perhaps our rites, like the sign of peace, should embody that disjuncture by providing a little discomfort for Christians and for those watching to 'see how those Christians love another another.'

Theology: This matter has implications for liturgical practice today. Since the reform of liturgy, the time for the exchange of the peace is one of the matters that does not seem to have been settled comfortably. The letter of Innocent has loomed large as one of the early historical precedents in the discussions of the placement of the peace in the Eucharistic liturgy.

Bearing the teaching of Jesus in the New Testament in mind in this regard, one thinks of his admonition, 'Before you bring your gift to the table, be reconciled to your brother and sister,' and perhaps this is the impetus behind early witnesses, like Innocent, who advocate that the sign of peace happen within the communion rite. Considering the ethical content of the structure of the Eucharist, we are mindful of the recitation of the 'Our Father' after the Eucharistic prayer, in which the assembly prays aloud together, 'And forgive us our trespasses as we forgive those who trespass against us.' The sign of peace after the Our Father and before the distribution of the bread and wine might have arisen from the scriptural and euchological traditions before the early fifth century.

There are advocates for moving the gesture who find, as many do, that the exchange of peace after the Eucharistic prayer and before distribution seriously interrupts the flow of the table rite. In communities where the peace is protracted and enthusiastic, we can witness the languishing of the just-consecrated bread and wine while the presider and the members of the assembly exchange the peace and sing about the gift of peace. In traditions that have moved the peace to another place in the Sunday Eucharist, it has usually been put in the opening rites, where it functions as a kind of 'get to know those standing nearby,' or after the sermon and before the procession of the gifts to the altar.

The few sentences from Innocent reveal that, even if not done so in the Church of Rome, some communities are familiar with the exchange of peace taking place only among the priests themselves. Current liturgical theology and practice are clear that the exchange of peace is not a ritual element that is to be reserved only for the participation of the clergy.

2
On the Recitation of Names

De nominibus vero recitandis antequam precem sacerdos faciat, atque eorum oblationes quorum nomina recitanda sunt sua oratione commendet quam superfluum sit, et ipse pro tua prudentia recognoscis, ut cuius hostiam necdum Deo offeras, eius ante nomen insinues, quamvis illi incognitum nihil sit. Prius ergo oblationes sunt commendandae, ac tunc eorum nomina quorum sunt edicenda, ut inter sacra mysteria nominentur, non inter alia quae ante praemittimus ut ipsis mysteriis viam futuris precibus aperiamus.

About the recitation of names before the priest recites the prayer and commends in his prayer the offerings of those whose names have been recited: Your own discernment would have you see how foolish it is not to offer the sacrifice to God until you have mentioned someone's name, since God knows everything. The sacrifice is therefore offered up first, and then comes the names of those who have brought them. This is done so that the names are mentioned within the sacred rites and not among the other things that happen earlier. In this way we clear the path for these very rites in future prayers.

Textual variants: In the previous paragraph we had seen that *precem*, meaning 'prayer,' had been used in place of *pacem*, meaning 'peace,' in the other manuscripts. Here in the paragraph on the recitation of the name, the same words are transposed in five or six manuscripts but in the opposite direction, *pacem* or *pace* or *pacis*, all meaning 'peace,' has been used in place of *precem*, 'prayer.' The paragraph about the 'peace' in Innocent's letter signals that the place of the sign of peace in the Eucharistic liturgy was not the same in all churches, and the diversity of practice of course precipitated his address to this issue. The substitution of the words for 'peace' and 'prayer' in some of the manuscripts is not, then, a surprise, but it does leave us uncertain today about the variety of ritual order and practices in the Eucharist in the early fifth century.

Another consequential substitution in this paragraph is when the scribes put 'ordination' in place of 'oration' at the end of the first sentence, thereby making 'in his prayer he favours the offerings' into 'in his ordination he favours the offerings.' Although there are five manuscripts with this change, they are of the same lineage and therefore the change was made by one and then copied from it by four or five scribes. Perhaps the initial variant may have been favoured for a rite of ordination in a certain community of faith.

Key words: That the word *precem*, 'prayer,' in the first sentence clearly refers to what we presently call the 'Eucharistic prayer' is clear from the other words in the discussion: 'offering,' 'oblation,' 'sacred rites,' 'these very mysteries.'

History: The issues at hand in this paragraph are, in particular, acknowledging the members of the assembly who have provided the offerings for the Eucharist and, in general, on fixing a formula for the Eucharistic rite. On the former we cannot be sure if Innocent is writing of monetary support of the Church and its liturgy or if he writes of those who literally made the bread and the wine for the Eucharist. If the offering was indeed monetary, the practice must have needed some guidance or direction because the New Testament itself has numerous places, in the gospels and letters, where favouring the rich over the poor in the liturgical assembly is rebuked. In his First Letter to the Corinthians, for example, Paul writes about the difference in the community's treatment of the rich members and the poor members. Moreover, the Letter of James similarly rebukes the rich for not providing for the needs of the poor in the community.

On the fixed formula for the Eucharist, we see in Innocent's concern the Roman inclination toward uniformity in the prayer structure. As with all the matters Innocent takes up in the letter, so here too his concern is born from diversity rather than consensus. In the early fifth century the Church had not yet mandated exact formulas for the Eucharistic prayers, and certainly not until the revision of the rites in the sixteenth century, after the invention of the printing press, such a feat have been possible universally. In spite of this, the paragraph on the recitation of names indicates that there is a growing concern with the structure of the prayer and its theology.[25]

Theology: Oral and liturgical traditions would certainly give a rhetorical and theological shape to the Eucharistic prayer but the medium for exact prescription does not emerge until printing makes the reproduction of an approved text possible. A papal prescription for exact wording of the prayer was still a millennium away when Innocent I writes to Bishop Decentius; nevertheless, there is clearly a concern in this period of change that the theological and liturgical elements have a consonance from church to church in their basis shape and meaning. This letter is one of the earliest pieces of evidence for the concern over the ordering of the elements of the Roman Eucharistic prayer.

Innocent's recommendation raised the issue of how tightly prescribed should the Eucharistic prayer be and how tied to the text and order need each particular assembly be? Innocent's letter reveals that there was indeed a variety of practices, and so one is left wondering if there is a precedent for a parish's reworking of the Eucharistic prayer according to its experience of the presence of God and its experience as the body of Christ realized in a particular place, time, culture. To that end do those who have contributed financially to a parish and to the parish's worship have priority in the rites themselves by having their names included in the prayer?

---

25   Allan Bouley, *From Freedom to Formula: The Evolution of the Eucharistic Prayer from Oral Improvisation to Written Texts* (Catholic UP, Washington DC, 1981).

3
On the Signing of Infants

De consignandis vero infantibus manifestum est non ab alio quam ab episcopo fieri licere. Nam presbyteri licet sint sacerdotes, pontificatus tamen apicem non habent. Hoc autem pontificibus solis deberi, ut vel consignent, vel paracletum Spiritum tradant non solum consuetudo ecclesiastica demonstrat, verum illa lectio actuum apostolorum quae asserit Petrum et Iohannem esse directos qui iam baptizatis tradant Spiritum sanctum. Nam presbyteris seu extra episcopum sive praesente episcopo cum baptizant, chrismate baptizatos unguere licet, sed quod ab episcopo fuerit consecratum, non tamen frontem ex eodem oleo signare, quod solis debetur episcopis cum tradunt Spiritum paracletum. Verba vero dicere non possum, ne magis prodere videar quam ad consultationem respondere.

Regarding the signing of infants, this clearly cannot be done validly by anyone other than the Bishop. For even though presbyters are priests, none of them holds the office of pontiff. For not only is it ecclesiastical custom that shows this should be done only by pontiffs—in other words, that they alone would sign or give the comforting Spirit—but there is also that reading in the Acts of the Apostles that describes Peter and John being ordered to give the Holy Spirit to those who had already been baptized. For whether the Bishop is present or not, presbyters are allowed to anoint the baptized with chrism. But they are not allowed to sign the forehead with the same oil consecrated by the Bishop, for that is used by the bishops only when they give the Spirit, the Paraclete. I cannot reveal the words themselves, lest I seem to betray more than is needed to respond to your inquiry.

Textual variants: What is clear in considering the textual variants on this particular topic is that many of the scribes were particularly attentive to the establishing precisely the kind and number of the ministers for the anointing rite, particularly with references to the ecclesial offices and orders. Some scribes edited language about 'pontiffs,' which would suggest perhaps that such an office could be held by several persons at the same time, and some changed the word to refer to 'pontifical office,' rendering indeterminable the number of persons, singular or plural, who might be in the office.

In this regard we might be reminded that Innocent's episcopate was very much in a period during which the office of the Bishop of Rome was in transition from being one *pontificatus* among others—i.e., in other major churches in the Christian world—to being considered the only *pontificatus*, and the one, by Innocent's own reckoning, to whom other bishops would turn in times of trouble or when needing counsel. There is one manuscript that changed the first appearance of 'bishop' to 'bishops,' but in general the groundswell of editing was directed to variants regarding the word 'pontiff.'

Key words: As in later issues taken up in the letter, much attention was put into precision regarding what ministers were performing what aspects of the rites, indicating thereby some uncertainty in this period of the 'awe-inspiring rites of initiation.' Although there is some uncertainty about what office were being intended with the words, in the translation above we have used the English words literally closest to the Latin. So 'bishop' is for *episcopus*, 'presbyter' for *presbyterus*, 'priest' for *sacerdos*, and 'pontiff' for *pontifex*.

The very distinction here between the responsibilities that can be done in the rites by the *presbyterus* and what by the *sacerdus* is key in recognizing that there was some fluidity from place to place in these matters. The last sentence of this section reveals clearly that Decentius had a particular inquiry about the anointing, and his Church, at the crossroads of four major metropolitan territories, was not sure about the liturgical roles of the various ecclesial ministries.

Some commentators have thought that Innocent's use of the word 'infants' in the first sentence of the section is referring not literally to small children but, rather, in a metaphorical way to those who have been newly born in faith—i.e., adults who have recently been baptized, or, as we call them today, the 'neophytes.' This is certainly a possibility, but nothing in the text suggests a translation other than the literal, 'infants.'

Another vocabulary distinction of the section is between the two words for 'anointing.' As with the ministries, we have translated the Latin with transliteration where possible. So *consignare* is rendered as 'to sign,' *unguere* as 'to anoint,' and the nouns *oleum* as 'oil' and *chrisma* as 'chrism.' At the start, in the first phrase, 'regarding the signing of infants,' Innocent uses *consignandis*, those who are to be marked ('-signed') together ('con-'). Later, however, when he writes that 'presbyters are permitted to anoint the baptized with chrism,' different words are used. Here he does not use *consignandis*, which etymologically does not necessarily suggest the use of oil, but *unguere*, which does literally mean 'to anoint.' Yet the noun of the same sentence is 'chrism.' Perhaps the change of references is tied to the change of the liturgical minister who does the anointing—i.e., the bishop is 'marking together,' while the presbyter is merely 'anointing.' But there are too many variables to know the reasons for the vocabulary shifts.

History: The indictment of biblical studies—'never has so much been written about so little'—would not be untrue regarding this section of Innocent's letter to Bishop Decentius. For many who have studied the rite of anointing as a discrete sacrament of initiation (with baptism and Eucharist), a rite which comes to be known centuries later as the 'sacrament of confirmation,' this short paragraph from Innocent has been utilized as an early liturgical warrant.

Innocent's ascription of the anointing as a ritual action only for the bishops has come to be seen as a ministerial distinction as much as a ritual one. Moreover, Innocent's own appeal to a warrant in the Acts of the Apostles adds more weight for advocates of this view because it can seem to suggest that it was an unbroken tradition from the late first century to the fifth, and, with that as a precedent, from the fifth century to our own time. Indeed some who have written about this paragraph and cited this letter in their arguments refer to the section itself as being 'On Confirmation,' even though the word 'confirmation' does not appear in the original Latin.

Theology: We have already considered the influence of polemical theological and social contexts on the shape of the liturgy, and on the emergence of the Triduum in particular. Aidan Kavanagh posited that some of what contributes to this section of Innocent's letter is also the influence of a polemical theological issue, here on the divinity of the Holy Spirit.[26] Of the many theological issues raised in the theological councils of the fourth and fifth centuries, the role and divinity of the Holy Spirit was at hand in the latter half of the fourth century. As he considered the addition of the role of the Holy Spirit in the hand-laying and dismissal rites, Kavanagh marks the change in Roman initiatory prayers from the anointing prayer addressed earlier to 'Lord God' and later to the Holy Spirit. Kavanagh sees the theological controversies regarding the divinity and relative equality of the Holy Spirit in relation to the Father and the Son as an impetus to the insertion of the Holy Spirit in a prayer where earlier this had been absent.[27]

Moreover, in this section of Innocent's letter do we find the first use of Acts 8 as a proof-text for the anointing in the early church. First, let us consider the passage itself (8.14-17):

'Now when the apostles at Samaria had accepted the word of God, they sent Peter and John to them. The two went down and prayed for them that they might receive the Holy Spirit (for as yet the Spirit had not come upon any of them; they had only been baptized in the name of the Lord Jesus). Then Peter and John laid hands on them, and they received the Holy Spirit.'

Although this text supports the notion that the reception of the Holy Spirit might be temporally at a remove from baptism, there are other New Testament passages about baptism in which the gift of the Holy Spirit is clearly linked to baptism, with some, Kavanagh asserts, narrating that 'the Holy Spirit came upon his [Peter's] hearers *before* their baptism rather than after it.'[28] Among these other passages Kavanagh mentions Acts 10.44-48 and 11.14-18, and thereby does he indict Innocent's use of Acts 8 as 'selective.' What Innocent contributes to subsequent interpretations of the anointing rite and to later theologies of the minister of the sacrament of confirmation are the notions that the advent of the Holy Spirit could be temporally removed from initiation and that there is a precedent for this in the passage from Acts 8.

26 See his *Confirmation: Origins and Reform* (Pueblo, New York, 1988) pp 52-64.
27 See page 59 in particular; the 'Verona' version of *Apostolic Tradition* 21 is laid out in parallel with the later version in the Gelasian Sacramentary. The emendation of 'send upon them your grace' so that it becomes 'pour upon them, Lord, your Holy Spirit, the Paraclete' can, according to Kavanagh, be at least partially attributable to the pneumatological questions being discussed in the second half of the fourth century and the first part of the fifth century.
28 Kavanagh, page 57.

Another problem with Innocent's use of Acts 8 is that this passage describes the role of the Holy Spirit as linked to the apostles Peter and John's laying hands on those who had already been baptized while the ritual action in Innocent's letter is not hand-laying but anointing with oil. So it is clear that Innocent is selective in not only excising this passage away from others in Acts that provide a contrary witness but also in taking what he finds necessary, the separation of the gift of the Holy Spirit from baptism, and applies it to another ritual action.

Moreover, Kavanagh imputes to Innocent a dependence on the rhetoric of 'ecclesiastical custom' even though he is introducing a ritual meaning to the custom for which there is no earlier evidence. Kavanagh is gentle in describing Innocent's use of the action and addition of a new meaning as a kind of inculturation, or, in Kavanagh's own words, as 'a good example of bending liturgy to serve theology and current pastoral needs.' In the end, he describes Innocent's contribution in this regard as one 'making it seem as though the Holy Spirit had to be supplied *after* baptism by a second post-baptismal anointing *in frontem* at episcopal hands.' Given the ecclesial, social, and military context of Innocent's place and time, we can certainly understand Innocent's desire to straiten the discipline of the rites and the precise liturgical responsibilities of the Bishop in ordering the Church. But seeing, in retrospect, the influence that Innocent's reworking of the anointing would eventually have for the sacrament of confirmation, one can lament his skilful inculturation of this liturgical element.

In his work *The Rites of Christian Initiation* Maxwell Johnson has closely interpreted the Western rites of initiation in the early period.[29] Therein he examined the rite of the anointing in the *Apostolic Tradition*, a church order of the early third century (ca. 215) attributed to Hippolytus, a series of rites thought by many to have been used in the Church of Rome. Indeed for many the *Apostolic Tradition* is the source on which the present restoration of the rites of initiation in the RCIA depends.

Looking at the *Apostolic Tradition* juxtaposed to what is described by Innocent in this section, we find that, like Innocent, Hippolytus is marked in distinguishing the ritual acts of the presbyter from those of the Bishop:

'The neophytes are anointed by the presbyter from the oil consecrated by the Bishop. He says, "I anoint you with holy oil in the name of Jesus Christ." And thus, drying themselves, the individuals are vested, and afterwards are brought in the Church.

'And the Bishop, imposing his hand on them, prays by saying, "Lord God, who made them worthy to merit the forgiveness of sins by the bath of rebirth of the Holy Spirit, send your grace onto them, that they may serve you according to your will. For to you is the glory, to the Father and

---

29 Maxwell E. Johnson, *The Rites of Christian Initiation: Their Evolution and Interpretation* (Liturgical Press, Collegeville, 1999) pp 130.

to the Son with the Holy Spirit in the holy Church, both now and for ever. Amen."

'Afterwards, pouring the consecrated oil from his hand and imposing it on the neophyte's head, let him say, "I anoint you with holy oil in the Lord, the Father Almighty, and Christ Jesus, and the Holy Spirit,"

'And consigning the neophyte on the forehead, let him offer the kiss and say, "The Lord be with you." And let those who have been signed say, "And also with you." Let him do the same to each individual.'[30]

It is clear that, two centuries before Innocent's letter, there were two anointings in the Roman initiation rite, one by the presbyter using 'oil consecrated by the bishop,' and after the episcopal hand-laying, another by the bishop. This too is 'consecrated oil,' but the text does not make it readily clear if the source of the oil used by the presbyter and the bishop is the same.

We can tell from Innocent's letter that some presbyters must have been usurping the episcopal role in the anointing: 'This can be done by none other than the bishop.' Mindful of the fourth of Paul Bradshaw's ten principles for intepreting early Christian liturgical evidence—'Legislation is better evidence for what it proposes to prohibit than for what it seeks to promote'—we can be sure that presbyters were indeed making chrism and anointing with it, Innocent's insistence on restraining the ritual action to the bishop clarifies that presbyters were surely anointing and perhaps Decentius's letter of inquiry addressed this in particular.[31]

Paul Turner has written a handy compendium of texts in *Sources of Confirmation from the Father through the Reformers*.[32] Of note for the present consideration are the papal texts about the post-baptismal anointing promulgated from Rome in the centuries just after Innocent's papacy. Less than a century after Innocent's letter is a letter from Pope Gelasius, Bishop of Rome from 492 to 496. About the anointing he wrote:

'Nor any less do we prohibit presbyters to extend their limit farther, nor boldly to take on themselves the things reserved to the episcopal degree: not to seize for themselves the faculty for making chrism nor of applying the pontifical consignation. Neither should they presume permission for themselves to supply prayers or sacred actions when a bishop is not present, unless they were perhaps commanded. Nor may they presume to sit within his sight, unless commanded, nor to enact the sacred mysteries.'[33]

Certain liturgical actions, such as this last, the 'enacting of the sacred mysteries,' are never permitted for the presbyters, but others are permitted

---

30 Original text in *Sources Chrétiennes* 11bis: 86-90; translation here from Paul Turner, *Sources of Confirmation from the Father through the Reformers* (Liturgical Press, Collegeville, 1993) pp 12-13.

31 Paul F. Bradshaw, *The Search for the Origins of Christian Worship: Sources and Methods for the Study of Early Liturgy* (Oxford UP, New York, 1992) pp 59-79, here at 68-70.

32 (Liturgical Press, Collegeville, 1993).

33 As in PL 59:50; translation from Turner, #104, page 56.

when the requisite permission has been obtained. Among these latter seems to be the consignation. This did not put the issue to rest, for about a century later it is taken up by Pope Gregory the Great in two letters. The first is letter 9, written in 593:

> 'Presbyters should not presume to sign baptized infants on their foreheads with sacred chrism. But presbyters may anoint the baptized on the breast, so that afterwards bishops may confirm on the forehead.'[34]

And just a year later, clearly in response to objections about the former, was written still another, this letter 26 to Januarius:

> 'It has also come to our attention that some people were scandalized that we prohibited presbyters to anoint those who have been baptized with chrism. And indeed we have done this according to the ancient custom of our Church. But if any are troubled at all by this, we concede that where bishops are absent, even presbyters ought to anoint the baptized with chrism on their foreheads.'[35]

So what are we to make of this volley of texts regarding the role of the presbyter and the role of the bishop in the anointing rites of Rome? Because there is such a wide gap between the *Apostolic Tradition* of 215 and Innocent's letter two centuries later, we are reliant only on what Decentius tells the Church in the letter as indicative of the novel pressures or concerns. To that end we see in his insistence on the necessary role of the leader of the community that the bishop's role is one of stability, a key symbolic component in the context of the conquering of the city by the northern Germanic tribes, under their king Alaric. The bishop, as leader of the Church, could provide a foundation to assure an ecclesial and ritual continuity in the midst of social and economic strife, and this desire for stability is what contributes to Innocent's forthright statement, 'This is to be done by none other than the bishop.'

Yet there is also the ecclesial factor of more and more initiations as Christianity becomes the most popular religion and the one that might be socially most advantageous as well. While there are too many factors contributing to the shift in ritual responsibilities to discern how much each factor contributed, we know, first, that the world outside the Church had changed dramatically; second, that there were more and more persons seeking to become Christian; third, that the authority of the character of the bishop was a mark of stability in an otherwise unstable period; that the availability of the bishop for each initiation would be less and less likely as time passed. Innocent takes up the side of the bishop as the sole minister of the post-baptismal anointing; Gelasius and Gregory have sought to modify this when they write that, with requisite permission from their bishops, presbyters too can administer the anointing using the oil consecrated by the bishop.

---

34 Turner, #108.
35 Turner, #109.

4
On the Saturday Fast

Sabbato vero ieiundandum esse, ratio evidentissima demonstrat. Nam si diem dominicum ob venerabilem resurrectionem domini nostri Iesu Christi non solum in Pascha celebramus, verum etiam per singulos circulos hebdomadarum ipsius diei imaginem frequentamus, ac sexta feria propter passionem domini ieiunamus, sabbatum praetermittere non debemus, qui inter tristitiam atque laetitiam temporis illius videtur inclusus. Nam utique constat apostolos biduo isto et in moerore fuisse et propter metum Iudaeorum se occuluisse. Quod utique non dubium est in tantum eos ieiunasse biduo memoratur, ut traditio ecclesiae habeat, isto biduo sacramenta penitus non celebrari. Quae forma utique per singulas hebdomadas est tenenda propter id quod commemoratio diei illius semper est celebranda. Quod si putant semel atque uno sabbato ieiunandum ergo et dominicum et sexta feria semel in Pascha erit utique celebrandum. Si autem dominici diei ac sextae feriae per singulas hebdomadas reparanda imago est, dementis est bidui agere con-suetudinem sabbato praetermisso, cum non disparem habeat causam, a sexta videlicet feria, in qua dominus passus est quado et ad inferos fuit ut die tertia resurgens rederet laetitiam post biduanam praecedentem tristitiam. Non ergo nos negamus sexta feria ieiundandum, sed dicimus et sabbato hoc agendum quia ambo dies tristitiam apostolis vel his qui

Reason clearly indicates that Saturday should indeed be a day of fasting. For if we celebrate the Lord's day because of the sacred resurrection of our Lord Jesus Christ, we do so not only at Easter but also on the image of that day in the weekly cycle. Then surely we should frequently observe that other day throughout the cycle of each week also, for if we fast on Friday because of the passion of the Lord, we should not overlook Saturday, which is enclosed between the time of sadness and the time of rejoicing. For during those two days the apostles were in mourning and were hiding out of fear of the Jews. Let there be no doubt, then, about commemorating by fasting during these two days, because the tradition of the Church maintains that the sacraments are strictly not to be celebrated in this two-day span. This shape is to be observed every week so that the memory of this day will be forever celebrated. If some think that they should fast only once and that this be on Saturday alone, then the celebration of Sunday and of Friday will happen only at Easter. Yet if the memory of Sunday and of Friday are to be restored for each week, then they are crazy who observe the customs of those two days but overlook Saturday, whose purpose is no different from what happens on those two days. For Friday is observed because it was on this day that the Lord suffered and went to the dead world so that, rising on the third day, he might restore the joy after the two days

34

Christum secuti sunt indixerunt. Qui die dominica hilarati non solum ipsum festivissimum esse voluerant, verum etiam per omnes hebdomadas frequentandum esse duxerunt.

of sadness. We do not, then, deny that Friday should be a day of fasting, but we add that Saturday should be so also, for it is evident that on both days sadness overshadowed the apostles and those who had followed Christ. Those who rejoiced on the Lord's day wanted not only that it be very festive, but it be observed more frequently, which is every week.

Textual variants: Even though Innocent wrote more about the Saturday fast than about any of the other particulars of the liturgy, there is very little scribal variation on this topic. The only one of consequence is that three manuscripts, all of the same manuscript branch, omit the 'no' from the phrase 'whose purpose is no different from what happens on those two days,' when he is comparing the observance of Saturday to that already established on Friday and Sunday. The meaning for the readers of those three manuscripts would suggest, then, that the purpose of the Saturday observance 'is different from what happens on' Friday and Sunday.

Key words: The numbering and naming of days in fifth-century Rome was different from the names we use today in English. Friday is called the 'sixth day,' *sexta feria*, which is determined ordinally when Sunday is the first day, Friday is the sixth day; Saturday is called the 'sabbath,' as we might expect from the biblical tradition; and Sunday (and also Easter) is called the 'Lord's day' or the 'day of the resurrection.'

Though the earliest Christians used it to refer to Passover, the word *pascha* had for the first four centuries of Christianity traditionally referred to the annual celebration of Easter. The advocacy from Innocent that the annual observance of Easter is also to be observed weekly suggests that the *paschal* character of Easter is not applied to the observance of Sunday, and even to Friday and Saturday. The ancient traditions of what we call the 'Three Days,' the *triduum*, were in the fifth century being proposed as a weekly observance but probably not with the ritual intensity or longevity that is found in other churches, such as in Egeria's description of the rites in Jerusalem in the late fourth century. But Innocent is recommending that every Christian week would have its *triduum*, its own recounting of the events of the end of the life of Jesus of Nazareth and his followers.

Similar to the word *triduum* is *biduum*, which means 'two days.' In fact this paragraph from Innocent does not mention anything about a *triduum* but does repeatedly talk about the 'two days.' The two days about which he writes are of course Saturday and Friday, the days leading up to both the Easter feast and the Sunday assembly.

History: Attention to the chronology of the Gospels' accounts of the last days of Jesus of Nazareth did not follow immediately after the death of Jesus.

Expecting that the world as they knew it would not be lasting for long, the early Christians did not attend to the calendar as assiduously as we might imagine or as we ourselves do today. When such concerns emerged, Church leaders were not attending to the chronology of Jesus in order to relate it to the Christian week, but they attended to it because of disputes over the dating of the annual observance of Easter. Different dates for marking Easter are on the record books from the late second century until today. Innocent's letter, however, is not addressing a needed change in the annual cycle but one that would be applied to the weekly cycle and how the regular Sunday observance is to be anticipated by fasting on Friday and Saturday.

Keeping fasts each week was not original to Innocent or to the Church of Rome. There is evidence for a concern about weekly observances of fasts from the earliest literature after the New Testament. The church order known as the *Didache*, a witness to church life in a late-first- or early-second-century community, testifies to fasting on Wednesdays and Fridays. This witness to weekly fasting on Wednesdays and Fridays is confirmed by Tertullian, the North African writer whose work *De ieiunio*, 'On Fasting,' is the earliest Christian text explicitly attending to fasting practices, and it was written around 215 CE. Tertullian's writing suggests that the annual fast in anticipation of Easter was the only universal observance of fasting. The weekly fasts were not communal but according to the piety of individuals. A rigorist in many ways, Tertullian commends the personal observance of fasting on Wednesdays and Fridays. He is clear that this weekly observance is not apostolic in origin; only the annual paschal fast is from the apostles. Because the recommendation of fast days from Tertullian is for Wednesday and Friday, it does not seem to be connected to the chronology of the passion of Jesus as is the recommendation of Innocent in the letter.

We do not know, from Innocent's letter or from another Roman source contemporary with Innocent's episcopate, exactly in what the fast referred to consisted. But we can tell—from the imperative tone of the Bishop's teaching and from the appeal, once again, to the witness of the behaviour and feelings of the apostles themselves—that Innocent knew this was not or would not be observed readily by the community under Decentius's guise.

We can recall at this point the pope's appeal, at the opening of this letter, to the sure witness of the apostles and to the unwavering liturgical traditions that have been maintained from that time. Back there, in the first few sentences of the letter, Innocent pointed out the 'church customs that have been handed down from the blessed apostles,' which he highlights in order to pose that 'there should be no diversity, no variety in the rites and blessings.' In many of the writings of the early church, an advocate for a tradition being questioned or, perhaps, slowly being superseded by the introduction of some new practice would immediately appeal to the authority of the apostles. This apostolic appeal was not unique, really, because in many of the debates of the first few centuries both sides appealed to the apostolic precedent for what they were advocating.

Because the liturgical celebrations of the Easter Triduum—the 'three days' from Holy Thursday to Easter Sunday—have undergone a successful renewal in the past few decades, most Christians presume that these traditions go back indeed to the time of the apostles and Jesus of Nazareth or, at least, to the time of the writing of the gospel narratives. But in fact there is no evidence for the *triduum* before the second half of the fourth century.[36]

Immediately after the death of Jesus, virtually all those confessing Jesus as the Messiah were Jews, and therefore their main annual observance was not Easter but Passover. Indeed in the First Letter to the Corinthians (5.7), when the apostle Paul writes of the paschal lamb that has been sacrificed, he is drawing primarily from the Jewish ritual tradition which, for followers of the 'new way,' was gradually being applied to Jesus of Nazareth.

Passover was celebrated on a calendar date (14 Nisan) for about two centuries before there would be an impetus to have it celebrated on a Sunday. The move toward having the annual observance on Sunday marks the increasing autonomy of Christianity as a separate cult, for in the same period we hear from many Christian leaders anti-Jewish rhetoric and a theology in which the Christians presume that Christianity is indeed displacing the theology and practices of the Jews. This theological tradition is often called a supercessionary theology, with Christians thinking that their traditions would 'supercede' the tradition of the Jews.

Once there is a blending of the weekly observance of Sunday and the annual observance of Easter, the result is that the annual liturgical customs are moved to a Sunday. Evidence of this struggle between those advocating Easter on a Sunday and those 'Judaizers' (also called 'Quartodecimans,' a name taken from the Latin word for 'fourteen,' from the date 14 Nisan) who wanted to stick to the date in the calendar rather than the day of the week is found in the letter of Pope Victor (in 170 CE). It would still be another two centuries before the tradition of celebrating Easter on a Sunday evolves into the three-day observance from Holy Thursday to Easter Sunday.

We find this first in the diary of Egeria, of 383 CE, a chronicle written while she was visiting Jerusalem. And, in the West in the same period, we find evidence of the *triduum* in the writings of Ambrose, Bishop of Milan (from 374-397). So the time in which Innocent is writing about the celebration of Easter is just a few decades after the invention of the *triduum*, and probably a time when not all churches had received the new liturgical temporal observance. What we find in the letter suggests that the annual observance was so 'successful,' at least to Innocent, that he has become an advocate of marking it every week. This would no longer be 'three days' of every cycle of 365 days, but 'three days' of every cycle of seven!

---

36 Martin Connell, 'Heresy and Heortology in the Early Church: Arianism and the Emergence of the Triduum' in *Worship* 72 (1998) pp 117-140.

Some have called the annual practice of following the narratives of the passion and resurrection during the Triduum a kind of 'historicization' of the liturgy. By this they have meant that churches were becoming more attentive to the scriptural details of the life of Jesus and to imitating these details in the liturgy and in their lives. Such imitation was possible in place only after the sites of the life of Jesus were established in the early fourth century. Consequent to the establishment of *place* was the concentration on *time*, on establishing the calendar of Jesus' life. Nascent in Jerusalem and Milan, the Triduum catches on rather quickly and is omnipresent in Christendom within a few decades. The theological question such an inclination might evoke, about the past and even about the present, is whether the tendency to unearth the details of the historical Jesus would impede the pastoral recognition of the life of the risen Christ in the life of the Church in the present.

Here in this section of Innocent's letter we find that the impetus toward following the chronology of Jesus' passion was not only prompting churches to observe such a schedule at the time of its annual *pascha*, but that Innocent is recommending that the chronology be observed every week. If once a year is good, his prescription might suggest, then once a week would be even better!

Theology: The area of pastoral theology that is most strongly impacted by this discussion of fasting is Christology. How does the local assembly participate in the life of Jesus of Nazareth? How does it participate in the body of Christ? Is it by the imitation of the chronology of the life of Jesus of Nazareth as this is recorded in the gospels? How does the Church keep in view the line between a balanced interest in the incarnate Saviour in first-century Palestine and the celebration of the risen Christ in the Church's time and place today?

It is a common hypothesis that worship in the fourth century shifted toward more attention to the historical life of Jesus, to the places in Palestine where the life of Jesus was lived, and, from the witness of Pope Innocent and from other fourth- and fifth-century witnesses, to the chronology of that life. The key pastoral issue is in coming to terms with the character of *imitation*. Why are the weekly fasts of Friday and Saturday so important to Innocent? Is it from their impact on the holiness on the discipline, holiness, and works of charity which flow from the observance? Or is it enough that the individuals of the community do what Jesus did?

5
On the Fermentum

De fermento vero quod die dominica per titulos mittimus, superflue nos consulere voluisti, cum omnes ecclesiae nostrae intra civitatem sint constitutae. Quarum presbiteri, quia die ipsa propter plebem sibi creditam nobiscum convenire non possunt, idcirco fermentum a nobis confectum per acolitos accipiunt, ut se a nostra communione maxime illa die non iudicent separatos. Quod per parrochias fieri debere non puto quia nec longe portanda sunt sacramenta nec nos per cimeteria diversa constitutis presbiteris destinamus et presbiteri eorum conficiendorum ius habeant atque licentiam.

About the *fermentum*, which we send on Sunday by way of the titular churches, it is worthless to consult us in this matter for all of our churches are within the city. But the presbyters of these churches—who cannot assemble with us on this day because their people need them—receive from the acolytes the *fermentum* that we consecrated, so that they do not find themselves separated from our communion on that great day. I do not think that this needs to be done in the parishes because the sacraments are not to be carried far nor should we send presbyters through different cemeteries; moreover, the presbyters are themselves, by law and licence, able to consecrate.

Textual variants: There are no consequential textual variants in this section.

Key words: The passage itself makes it clear that the *fermentum* is a piece of the Eucharistic bread to be carried to a member of the church who was not able to be present for the consecration itself.

The *titulos*, or 'titular churches,' would be those without a residential bishop but still within the jurisdiction of the bishop. This section demonstrates that the communion with bread was extended to the titular churches as a sign of the unity they shared in the Church.

The *acolytos*, is that from which our word 'acolyte' comes, though the Latin word itself is from the Greek. Acolytes are those who serve at the altar, and in the Middle Ages there would emerge a rite for making such servers officially designated members of the Church. In our time the word is used to refer both to those designated as such through the rite, but also for parish altar servers, children and adults, who assist the parish in the celebration of the sacraments.

History: The issue of distance is very important to Innocent in what he describes, for he makes it clear that the sacraments are not to be transported over a great distance and that previously consecrated bread is not of the same ecclesial or sacramental importance as the bread that would be consecrated at the liturgy itself. If the presbyters can consecrate, Innocent assures the reader, they should choose this over distributing the sacraments celebrated in another community.

The *fermentum* was a piece of bread to be used only for the inclusion of those who were not able to be present for the Eucharist, but a priority is given to the action of communion in the liturgy over the consecrated bread outside the context of the assembly. Earlier sources indicate that in some communities the bread was taken home by the faithful who were present on Sunday so that on the days between the weekly assemblies they might commune with the Church in remembrance of the Eucharist celebrated the Sunday before and in anticipation of the Eucharist to be celebrated on the approaching Sunday.

Theology: The symbol of the *fermentum* is telling about the ecclesiology of the Church of Rome, which was united with its Bishop not only by intention but by sharing in the Eucharistic meal over space and time. Etymologically, it is thought that this piece broken off from the present Eucharist would be added and moulded into the bread of another liturgy in the same way that yeast, *fermentum,* is added to and moulded into the dough in the process of making bread. Indeed, *fermentum* is the word used by Jerome in the Vulgate as he translated the short parable of the Gospel of Matthew, 'The kingdom of heaven is like *yeast* that a woman took and mixed in with three measures of flour until all of it was leavened' (13.33). So, liturgically, the *fermentum* of the Bishop of Rome would have been 'mixed in with' the Eucharistic bread of the neighbouring communities, thereby leavening both the bread and the community by this sign of ecclesial connection and integration. Jungmann saw this ritual action as a reminder of the Eucharist as the *sacramentum unitatis,* the 'sacrament of unity.'[37]

Another issue raised by the section is that of the sacrament being taken to cemeteries. This section on the *fermentum* does not provide any more than the prohibition of priests taking the bread from the eucharist to the cemeteries, but we do not know what would have been happening in the cemeteries to warrant Innocent's proscription against the *fermentum* being taken there.

The clear theological and liturgical distinction made by Innocent's letter is that those who can attend the Eucharist ought to, but the sacrament of unity can be brought to those who were unable to attend that celebration. The *fermentum* is not available for convenience, only for cases of necessity.

---

[37] Joseph A. Jungmann, *The Mass of the Roman Rite,* trans. Francis A. Brunner (Four Courts, Dublin, 1955) volume 2, p 312.

6
On Demonic Possession

De his vero baptizatis qui postea a daemonio, vitio aliquo aut peccato interveniente, arripiuntur, quaesivit dilectio tua si a presbitero vel diacono possint aut debeant consignari. Quod hoc nisi episcopum praecipere non licet. Nam ei manus imponenda omnino non est nisi episcopus auctoritatem dederit id efficiendi. Ut autem fiat episcopi est imperare ut manus ei vel a presbitero vel a caeteris clericis imponatur. Nam quomodo id fieri sine magno labore poterit ut longe constitutus energumenus ad episcopum deducatur, cum si talis casus ei in itinere acciderit, nec perferri ad episcopum, nec referri ad sua facile possit?

About those possessed by a demon after baptism whether because of some vice or because of the coming of sin. You ask if they might be or should be signed by a presbyter or deacon. This is not permitted except by the Bishop's order. Under no circumstances should hands be laid on them unless the authority of the Bishop has permitted this to happen. Yet if it is to take place, it is on the order of the Bishop that a hand be laid on them either by a presbyter or by other clerics. For how, without tremendous effort, could it happen that one so signed as an *energumen* could be brought to the Bishop? In case of such an event along the way, might it happen that the *energumen* would be both unable to be brought to the Bishop and unable to return easily?

Textual variants: As with so many of the liturgical issues taken up in this letter, the variants do not so much reveal what actions were done performed but who is doing them or giving permission for them to be done by others. The section on demonic possession says far more about who is to be ministering the hand-laying than about the possession itself or about the rite being celebrated.

The 'by a priest or by a deacon' at the end of the first sentence of the paragraph has variants with 'by priests or deacons,' and 'unless the Bishop gives authority' is rendered as 'unless the bishops give authority' in one manuscript. According to the number of the agents, so do the verbs change some of the time. The need for the bishop's permission for this rite is emphasized here more than in any other liturgical prescription in the whole letter.

Of great consequence also is the word used in the manuscripts to describe the action performed by the priest or deacon, also at the end of the first sentence, which is rendered here as 'if they might be or should be if they might be or should be *signed* by a priest or a deacon.' The editor of the critical edition of this letter, Robert Cabié, has explained his decision to use *consignari*, as follows: 'The reading of the primary text is without a doubt *designari*, but this is foolish; *consignari* is a correction, but it is the only one that would fit the context.' Twelve manuscripts have *designari*, two have *assignari*, and one *signari*. None have Cabié's preferred reading, *consignari*, which renders the meaning as 'signed' or 'marked.'

This choice might at first appear of little consequence, but in the context of the letter as a whole, one finds that the verb *consignare* is used only three times, once here in the paragraph about ministry to those possessed by a demon and two times in the paragraph about the post-baptismal anointing of infants, a ritual action done by the Bishop. While the roots of the verbs are the same—*signari*—the prefixes are of consequence because of its use in rhetoric about confirmation.

Cabié's use of 'marked,' *designari*, as 'foolish' is strong. *Designari* is grammatically fitting as the passive infinitive, and it is rhetorically appropriate as well as a description of a ritual action that would 'mark' or segregate the possessed differently than the rest of the community. Moreover, Cabié's option, in place of the textual priority, for a reading that has so much liturgical, ecclesial, ministerial, and even ecumenical weight attached to it in the history and theology of what will become the 'sacrament'of confirmation is hasty at best.

Key words: The word *energumen* is not one with which we are familiar in church practice today, even with the restoration of the catechumenate and the process of initiation. It refers to one who is possessed by a demon or devil.

History: We do not know what ritual action the original letter was describing with its use of the verb *designare*, nor do we know for sure what led to Cabié's risky choice to displace that with *consignare* and its echoes in the rites of initiation to follow in centuries to come. Because its consequence was presumably to expel the demon from the already baptized believer, it was exorcistic and directed to the end of restoring the possessed believers to their baptismal state of incorporation into the Church.

From the first century's accounts of Jesus' healing ministry and his expelling demons from many who were possessed, we know that ministry to the possessed was not new in the tradition. And pre-baptismal exorcisms are present in the rites of initiation in church orders of the third, fourth, and fifth centuries.

The witness of the letter of Innocent I qualifies the earlier witnesses in two ways: first, this is a post-baptismal rite; and second, the ranks of order—bishop, priest, deacon—and their roles in the post-baptismal exorcism are minutely spelled out. Nowhere in the New Testament is there a witness to post-baptismal exorcism, and nowhere before the letter to Decentius is there such a detailed explanation of the order of authority in the exorcism. The signing (or marking) is to be done 'by a priest or a deacon,' and then only if it follows 'an order from the bishop himself.' And, as if that is not already clear enough, he reiterates the emphasis on the bishop's command—'Under no circumstances should hands be laid on them unless the authority of the bishop has enabled them to do so'—and, a sentence later, still one more time: 'It is on the order of the bishop that a hand be laid on them.' Historians recognize that such prescriptions are not evidence that these rules were being followed at the time when they appear, rather they bear witness to be broken, giving the very reason for the rule to have been spelled. This is especially so in a description like this in which the chain of authority and command is given three times in an otherwise relatively spare account.

Theology: The perplexity of the communities dealing with those who were both already baptized and acting contrary to the values and prescriptions of their church community and its leaders is tangible in this paragraph. Since this is the very period of the 'awe-inspiring' rites of initiation, the lapsing of those already baptized must have posed a serious theological and liturgical threat to the leaders and the community. One can almost hear them asking, 'Were not the rites of initiation, the catechumenate, the mystagogy, and the wedding of the baptized person into the body of Christ efficacious? How could this person have been through the rites and still be acting so contrary to the life of the Church?' The process of initiation has exorcisms and prayers for expelling demons in it, but the section in Innocent's letter is explicitly dealing with the rite for those so possessed 'after' (*postea*) baptism. It is connected, therefore, to the subject of the next section, on penance.

On Penance

De paenitentibus autem qui sive ex gravioribus commissis sive ex levioribus paenitentiam gerunt, si nulla intervenit aegritudo, quinta feria ante Pascha eis remittendum Romanae ecclesiae consuetudo demonstrat. Caeterum de pondere aestimando delictorum sacerdotis est iudicare ut attendat ad confessionem paenitentis et ad fletus atque lacrimas corrigentis ac tunc iubere dimitti cum viderit congruam satisfactionem. Sane si quis aegritudinem inciderit atque uque ad desperationem devenerit, ei est ante tempus Paschae relaxundum ne de saeculo absque communione discedat.

About those who are doing penance for serious or venial sins, as long as they do not get sick, it is the custom of the Church of Rome to forgive their sins on the Thursday before Easter. It is the task of the priests to judge the seriousness by paying attention to the confession of the penitent and to the degree of correction needed based on the penitent's weeping and tears. When he has seen adequate reparation, he orders that the sins be forgiven. Someone who has grown weak, however, and who has arrived at the point of complete despair, may be absolved before that time before Easter, a relaxing of the rule lest the sick person depart from this world without communion.

Textual variants: In these three sentences on penance, there are a few manuscripts that have telling variants which reveal something about church practices at the time. Two of them reveal different ways in which the liturgical year was observed. One scribe, for example, writing is in a ninth-century manuscript from Monte Cassino, qualifies the time reference to *quinta feria ante Pascha*, the 'Thursday before Easter,' with *quod est cena domini*, 'which is the Lord's supper.' From our vantage point this seems merely repetitious because we are today quite familiar with the liturgical marking of the last supper (and the Johannine footwashing [13.1-20]), but it had been only a few decades before Innocent's letter when first Good Friday and then Holy Thursday were introduced into the liturgical year. There had been no *Triduum*, 'three days,' for the celebration of Holy Week until the last quarter of the fourth century. This manuscript reveals that the Church was still catechizing about the introduction of the new narrative and liturgical elements for that Thursday before Easter Sunday, which we call 'Holy Thursday.'

Also in terms of the liturgical year, there is some variation in the rendering of the description of the absolution of sin *ante tempus Paschae*, 'before the time of Easter.' This reference to 'the time of Easter' is likely pointing to the 50-day period of the Easter, or *quinquagesima*, a tradition which in the early fifth century was not universal. It seems that, on the one side, some churches had never really received the temporal tradition of the fifty days, and that, on the other side, some had received the fifty-day period earlier but that the period was breaking up by the time of Innocent I.

The variants in the last sentence of this paragraph reveal some of the diversity in the traditions of the liturgical year and the fifty-day season of Easter. Two manuscripts render the time for absolution as *ante Pascha*, 'before Easter,' instead of 'before the time of Easter,' and one indicates a season, *ante tempus*, but drops the connection of this with Easter.

Key words: While there may have been a desire and tendency in the early fifth century toward universal observances in some liturgical and pastoral practices, this is clearly not so in the practice of penance. Innocent's qualification regarding penance that he was writing about the *Romanae ecclesiae consuetudo*, the 'custom of the Roman Church,' with no apologies or indications that he was describing it as such so that others would fall in line for imitation, would suggest that the practices of penance and reconciliation were fairly diverse and accepted as such. (Then as now, one expects, the practices of sin are still both universal and particular at the same time.)

Theology: The witness of Innocent's letter that has grave bearing on pastoral rites in our time is about whether reconciliation should be considered a sacrament in itself or whether it is in reality a rite of restoring a believer or community of believers to a sacrament already realized and celebrated in initiation, when, completely undeserved, they became members of the body of Christ and thereby attained the means of salvation in the Church. Sin breaks the tie with the community and reconciliation reconnects the believer, physically, socially, and spiritually, with the community of faith.

Reconciliation, then, is a rite related to baptism, or at least a rite to renew one's baptism and its gift of God's life in humanity. The clearest association of the fifth-century rite of reconciliation and baptism is in the link with Easter, for in the fifth century Easter was the most common time in the liturgical year for initiation. That the rite of reconciliation would take place on Holy Thursday would have been to restore in the sinner their baptismal state so that they would again be knitted into the community of faith, a community that was going to be receiving new members at the initiation rites of Easter.

The naming of reconciliation as one of the seven sacraments—in the thirteenth century by Peter Lombard and then Thomas Aquinas—was confirmed canonically at the Council of Trent (1545-1563). Even in the Lutheran liturgical tradition, there was some ambiguity about whether reconciliation (or penance) was a sacrament, for Luther himself considered it one of the sacraments when he indicted the Roman Catholic Church for its seven and reduced them to three for Lutherans: baptism, Eucharist, and penance.[38]

---

38 Martin Luther, 'Babylonian Captivity of the Church,' in *Three Treatises* (Fortress, Philadelphia, 1970) pp 132, 206-218.

8
On Ministry to the Sick

Sane quoniam de hoc sicuti de caeteris consulere voluit dilectio tua, adiecit etiam fiius meus Caelestinus diaconus in epistola sua esse a tua dilectione positum illud quod in beati apostoli Iacobi epistola conscriptum est: si infirmus aliquis in vobis est vocet presbiteros et orent super ipsum, unguentes eum oleo in nomine domini et oratio fidei salvabit laborantem et suscitabit illum dominus et si peccatum fecit, remittet ei. Quod non est dubium de fidelibus aegrotantibus accipi vel intelligi debere qui sancto oleo chrismatis perungui possunt quod ab episcopo confectum non solum sacerdotibus sed et omnibus uti christianis licet, in sua aut in suorum necessitate unguendum. Caeterum illud superfluum videmus adiectum, ut de episcopo ambigatur, quod presbiteris licere non dubium est. Nam idcirco presbiteris dictum est, quia episcopi, occupationibus aliis impediti, ad omnes languidos ire non possunt. Caeterum si episcopus aut potest aut dignum ducit aliquem a se visitandum, et benedicere et tangere chrismate sine cunctatione potest, cuius est ipsum chrisma conficere. Nam paenitentibus istud infundi non potest, quia genus est sacramenti. Nam quibus reliqua sacramenta negantur quomodo unum genus putatur posse concedi.

Moreover, because you[39] sought advice about this, as about other things, even my own son Celestine the deacon has himself written a letter about what you raised concerning the passage in the letter of the blessed apostle James: 'Let anyone among you who is sick call for the presbyters, who will prayer over the infirmed. Let the sick be anointed with oil in the name of the Lord, and the prayer of faith will save the one who suffers, and if sin has been committed, the Lord will raise up the sick and the sin will be forgiven.'[40] There is no doubt but that this ought to be received and understood as referring to the faithful who are ailing for they are able to be anointed with the holy oil of chrism, which has been made by the Bishop. In case of emergency, this anointing is permitted not only for priests but even for all Christians. We know that anything else that might be added would be superfluous, such as there being confusion concerning the Bishop regarding what is without a doubt able to be done by presbyters. The passage refers here to presbyters because the bishops, whose schedules are quite taken up with other things, are not able to go be with all who are sick. Still, if the Bishop is able to visit or is taken to someone who is worthy of it, let him whose very job it is to make chrism visit and bless and touch the sick with chrism without hesitation. Nonetheless, this which is a kind of sacrament cannot be poured on penitents. For how can you agree to offer this one kind of sacrament to those who are denied the rest?

39 Literally, 'your delight,' *dilectio tua*.
40 James 5.24.

Textual variants: A general observation regarding this paragraph on the anointing of the sick is that considerable attention is given to emending the spelling of the ordained offices—bishop, priest, and deacon—and to getting the correct number (singular or plural) when the tasks of the ordained are being addressed. The sentences in which the orders are mentioned have many more variants than do most of the other subjects. This suggests that there were some differences in the fifth century about the tasks proper to the ordained ministries of bishop, priest, and deacon. Closer study of the manuscript tradition in this regard would surely be a fruitful task, but beyond the scope of the present work.

Among the notable variants one finds five manuscripts that have a different translation of the text of the Letter of James. *si infirmus aliquis in vobis est vocet presbiteros* in most manuscripts is emended into *infirmatur quis in vobis inducat* in these five of the same stemma. Moreover, an eighth-century manuscript in Paris, likely to have been from Treves originally, omits a long part of the same quote from James, leaving out *et orent super ipsum, unguentes eum oleo in nomine domini*. Yet because the beginning of this phrase, *et orent*, is similar to the start of the next part of the sentence, *et oratio*, this is perhaps a scribal error rather than a suggestion of a variant in sacramental practice for the sick in the community.

About possible variations in liturgical practice revealed in the textual variants, we see that where the letter speaks of the bishop visiting, 'blessing and touching with chrism,' five manuscripts omit the 'touching,' and one manuscript substitutes 'anointing,' *unguere*, for the excised 'touching,' *tangere*.

Another, more telling, variant revelatory of liturgical practice is in the same sentence. Here, instead of writing that the bishop would 'visit and bless and touch the sick with chrism without hesitation,' *sine cunctatione*, the scribe wrote that the bishop would 'visit and bless and touch the sick with chrism without singing,' *sine cantatione*. Perhaps the scribe wanted the anointing rite to occur expeditiously or knew that the bishop had a terrible singing voice!

History: The Letter of James is a kind of proof text for the Roman Catholic tradition of the sacrament of the sick. This dependence on James (5.14-15) was likely given a strong impetus by the citation of the passage here, one of the earliest contributory witnesses to the practice of the sacrament of the sick.[41]

Theology: The most striking aspects of this part of the letter of Innocent attend to the oil used and to whose job it is to 'make' the chrism for the sacrament, whose job it is to administer the oil, and under what circumstances what persons of what order of the faithful are permitted to administer the sacrament. There is a link, of course, between the ministers and the use of oil in this rite and the ministers and the use of oil discussed about in the initiatory oil, chrism. It is not merely about getting the rite right; it is about what liturgical tasks are assigned to what offices in the Church. There is at least as much concern in this letter for the configuration of the liturgical ministers and ministries as there is with the proper celebration of the rite.

---

41 For a historical survey of the sacramental ministry to the sick, see Charles W. Gusmer, *And Your Visited Me: Sacramental Ministry to the Sick and the Dying* (Pueblo, New York, 1984, 1989); on the place of Innocent's letter in the history, see pp 14-21.

Conclusion

His igitur, frater carissime, omnibus quae tua dilectio voluit a nobis exponi prout potuimus respondere curavimus, ut ecclesia tua Romanam consuetudinem a qua originem ducit servare valeat atque custodire. Reliqua vero quae scribi fas non erat, cum adfueris interrogati poterimus edicere. Erit autem domini potentiae etiam id procurare ut et tuam ecclesiam et clericos nostros qui sub tuo pontificio divinis famulantur officiis bene instituas et aliis formam tribuas quam debeant imitari.

Datum XIIII kal. Apr., Theodosio augusto VII et Palladio viro clarissimo consulibus.

And so, dearest brother, we have taken care to respond, as we were able, to all the things you had wanted us to explain so that your Church might be made strong by serving and observing the Roman customs in which it finds its origin. I am not able to write about the remaining matters of your inquiry, and it would be better if we were able to speak about them when you visit. May the power of the Lord be with you as you care for your Church and the clerics who serve in the holy ranks under your pontificate. May you teach well and offer to others an example that they ought to follow.

Given on the fourteenth day of the Kalends of April [19 March] in 416, when Theodosius Augustus the Seventh and the well-known Palladius were consuls.

Textual variants, key words: There are no major variants here, but we find key words here the end of the letter, the vocabulary of the letter's introduction on the central place of the Roman Church in establishing the customs for other communities of faith. Innocent does write of Decentius's 'pontificate', so to some extent he does see a collaboration in the administration of the Church and its traditions of worship.

History and Theology: As at the beginning of the letter, Innocent here returns to his central theme about Rome as the place of the origin of the liturgical traditions of the Church. One wonders how in Innocent's reckoning this origin would be related to the Church's origins in the life of Jesus of Nazareth and in the scriptures, but we have only this claim about the origin in Rome without any reference to the place of the memory of Jesus or of the use of scripture as the foundation on which the liturgical traditions of the Church are built. The concentration on the proper roles assigned those involved in worship pervades the letter from the start, as does the rhetoric about the role of the Church of Rome as the foundation for the liturgical traditions. As before, the context of this argument in the time after the conquering of the city is key in understanding Innocent's rhetoric about worship in the Church.